Sowing the Seeds of Free Enterprise:

The Politics of U.S. Economic Aid in Africa

by

Richard Sincere

With Foreword by

Duncan W. Sellars

International Freedom Foundation

✩ ✩

✩ ✩

International Freedom Foundation

200 G Street, N.E., Suite 300

Washington, D.C. 20002

(202) 546-5788

Duncan W. Sellars, Chairman

Contents

About the Author

Richard E. Sincere, Jr., is a widely-traveled issues analyst and writer based in Washington, D.C. Educated at Georgetown University and the London School of Economics and Political Science, he is the author of *The Politics of Sentiment: Churches and Foreign Investment in South Africa* (1984; 2nd ed., 1987) and co-editor (with Zbigniew Brzezinski) of *Promise or Peril: The Strategic Defense Initiative* (1986), both published by the Ethics and Public Policy Center. His articles on foreign and defense policy issues have appeared in *America, Global Affairs, International Journal on World Peace, Journal of Civil Defense, Los Angeles Herald-Examiner, Millennium, Pittsburgh Post-Gazette, Strategic Review, This World, USA Today, Vital Speeches of the Day, The Washington Times,* and *The World & I.* His book reviews have appeared in the *International Freedom Review,* the quarterly scholarly journal on international affairs published by the International Freedom Foundation.

Foreword

Richard Sincere's important study could not be more timely. The debate on foreign aid is an old one, but recent events in Eastern and Central Europe, as well as in the Philippines and Central America, have given it a renewed urgency.

While Americans as a people have always been exceptionally generous in supporting private charitable causes, they have also shown a deep skepticism about the merits of federal government assistance to foreign nations. In the past much foreign aid went to governments or through governments and did little to help the people of the recipient countries. Some of it was misdirected to supporting grandiose projects to inflate the self-esteem of third world petty tyrants; some of it was used to subsidize counter-productive collectivist schemes, and some was skimmed into the pockets of corrupt bureaucrats. In Africa this misdirection is legendary.

But in recent years a new emphasis has emerged, one best summed up by the adage that if you give a starving man a fish you must continue to do so every day. But if you teach him *how* to fish, you have supplied him with the means to avoid starvation in the future. Since the Reagan administration this insight has been put into practice more widely. As Mr. Sincere puts in the title of his work, we are now "sowing the seeds of free enterprise" in nations where endemic poverty has been made more acute by governments wedded to socialistic theories and policies.

From time to time, of course, there will be a need for emergency relief and there we can be expected to rush in quantities of food and medicine in response to disasters — drought, war, earthquake, and so forth. In such cases we have learned that private charitable organizations rather than governments are usually the most effective channels for seeing to it that our aid gets to the people who need it that most.

Wherever possible, Mr. Sincere points out, our aid programs should actively promote democratic reforms, since both logic and experience support the conviction that in the long run political freedom and economic freedom are inseparable. It is here hat our efforts often run into strong resistance from autocratic regimes that sense that the rise of an entrepreneurial class inevitable undermines arbitrary rule. In such cases a prudential approach makes sense, since democratic structures often require time to evolve and mature. But we must never lose sight of our goals, and to the extent that we press forward with the promotion of economic freedom we are eroding the rationale of statism and laying the groundwork for democratic reforms. In this connection, Mr. Sincere rightly pays tribute to the understanding work being done by the Center for International Private Enterprise, sponsored by the U.S. Chamber of Commerce. Even with its limited budget, CIPE has a remarkable record of achievement.

Mr. Sincere offers precisely the right prescription for the success of future aid programs:

(1) grassroots economic reform, working through the informal sector and providing financial, legal, and moral support for small businesses that face obstacles erected by the state;

(2) broad deregulation. . . .

(3) privatization of large, state-owned enterprise; and

(4) the contractions of the state...revising of legal codes to protect property and encourage individual initiative.

What makes Mr. Sincere's work so compelling is that he does not simply remain in the domain of theory. He presents a careful case-study analysis of the concrete problems of seven sub-Saharan African countries: Botswana, Ivory Coast, Ghana, Kenya, Senegal, South Africa, and Swaziland.

The chapter of South Africa is particularly timely in the light of recent hopeful developments there. Instead of concentrating on economic penalties to pressure Pretoria to widen its democracy to encompass all citizens, we should, he suggests, be looking for ways to support the rising black entrepreneurial and middle class. Major social changes, such as those that are beginning to take shape in South Africa are much more likely to sail smoothly in a rising economic tide.

Mr. Sincere's clear-headed analysis, at once compassionate and realistic, is a major contribution to the debate about foreign aid. It deserves careful study by everyone who cares about building a more secure, more prosperous, and more humane world.

Duncan W. Sellars

February 28, 1990

Preface

Economic and political development is likely to be the preoccupation of the 1990s. As the decade opens, it appears that democracy and free enterprise have been given an unexpected new lease on life by the states of Central Europe that were, until the remarkable summer and fall of 1989, firmly in the grip of totalitarian socialism. One by one the members of the Warsaw Pact deposed their Communist regimes and proclaimed their intentions to open up the political process through free elections and the legalization of opposition parties and to cut back on centralized control of the economy. The sight of hundreds of thousands of protesters in Prague's Wenceslas Square, moving unmolested where twenty-one years earlier Soviet tanks had put a violent end to similar demands for liberalization — of East and West Germans dancing and drinking atop the Berlin Wall — of Lech Walesa addressing the U.S. Congress — of Imre Nagy's hero's funeral, thirty-three years after his execution as a traitor by the same Hungarian state that was now honoring him — all these evoked soaring optimism among people in the West, who had become resigned to the perpetual slavery of the peoples of the East.

Room for skepticism remains, of course. Mikhail Gorbachev, on whose watch all these changes are taking place, has made clear on numerous occasions his commitment to the Communist system and to the Marxist-Leninist principles that are its foundations. *Perestroika* is meant to strengthen Communism and make the Soviet bloc more resilient. While the democracy movements in Poland and Hungary may be genuinely responsible for the political changes that have taken place there, it is just as clear that the Kremlin had a hand in the fall of the governments in Bulgaria, Czechoslovakia, East Germany, and Romania. Moreover, rapid changes in previously ossified states induce instability and resurrect old animosities that for forty years have lurked beneath the glossy surface of "socialist brotherhood and unity." The Cold

War may be ended, but there is considerable room for caution and no reason in the West to let down its guard.

Similarly, halfway around the world in South Africa, where the apartheid system has also existed for the past four decades, the walls are coming down. F. W. De Klerk was elected president on September 6, 1989, and immediately demonstrated how different — in tone, style, and substance — he would be from his predecessor, P. W. Botha. De Klerk permitted peaceful demonstrations, on a scale not seen since the 1950s, to take place in Cape Town, Johannesburg, and Pretoria, despite the existence of emergency regulations making such marches illegal. He released from prison leaders of the African National Congress. He proclaimed several previously segregated residential areas to be open to people of all races, and declared his determination to negotiate a new constitutional dispensation with black leaders committed to peaceful change.

Elsewhere in Africa, whether under the prodding of structural adjustment programs imposed by the World Bank or the International Monetary Fund or for more indigenous reasons (such as dissatisfaction with socialism or frustration over the poor quality of aid from the Soviet bloc), states are loosening up controls over their economies. In Namibia, a constituent assembly is beginning to devise a new constitution for this former South African territory and, at a continental summit conference in Zaire, the leaders of the opposing sides in the civil war in Angola actually met face to face to discuss their country's future. A new democracy is emerging in Nigeria, Africa's demographic giant, after years of military rule.

In short, from Szczecin on the Baltic to Durban on the Indian Ocean, winds of change are sweeping the Old World. The United States is not in a position to direct this change, but it can assist it and participate in it. This book is meant to explore the ways in which this has been done and might be done in the near future. It looks specifically at the promotion of free enterprise through economic assistance in seven African countries by the U.S. Agency for International Development

(U.S. AID). By way of introduction, it examines what foreign aid is, what the current economic situation in Africa is, and what the Agency for International Development does. It ends with recommendations for improvement in AID's programs and suggestions for alternatives when AID may not be the best channel for promoting free enterprise.

A number of people who have assisted or encouraged me during this project deserve acknowledgement. First of all, Duncan Sellars of the International Freedom Foundation, who invited me to write this book, is due much thanks for his confidence and patience, as are his colleagues at IFF, Jeffrey Pandin and Joseph Gimenez. I am grateful to those people who took the time from their busy schedules to allow me to interview them, including Richard Bissell of the U.S. Agency for International Development, Mark Clack of Congressman Kweisi Mfume's office, former Assistant Secretary of State for African Affairs Chester Crocker, Robert "Bud" Hancock of Transformation International Enterprises, and John Sullivan of the Center for International Private Enterprise. Less formal conversations with Armistead Lee of Peaceful Progress in South Africa and Jim Martin of the Congress on Racial Equality (CORE) also proved useful and enlightening.

Several people provided research materials to me that I might not otherwise have found, including Richard George of Senator David Boren's staff, Mickey Harmon of the House Foreign Affairs subcommittee on Africa, Michael Johns of the Heritage Foundation, John Montgomery of the South Africa Foundation, and Stephen Von Oehsen of the Society for International Development.

Useful comments on the manuscript were provided by Ghanaian economist George Ayittey, Nick Eberstadt of the American Enterprise Institute, Ambassador Herman Nickel, Thor Ronay and Philip Nicolaides of the Foundation for Africa's Future, and John Sullivan of CIPE. Of course, the selection of facts and judgments remains my own, as is responsibility for any errors.

My hope is that this book will be circulated widely enough that policymakers and analysts will be moved to think about the changes in the world and what the United States can do to help create an environment in which economic development can raise the standards of living for all peoples, thus paving the way for greater political stability and the widening of opportunities for democratic self-governance.

Richard E. Sincere, Jr.
Washington, D.C.
January 1, 1990

Introduction

Americans have always been generous in their aid to poor people in Africa. Even before government assistance became commonplace, American citizens, through their churches and philanthropic foundations, had sent money, food, and clothing to Africa to alleviate the effects of poverty. American missionaries began churches and schools in Africa soon after the birth of the American republic itself. As early as the 1930s, American foundations were supporting research about poverty in southern Africa, and making policy recommendations to the U.S. and colonial governments.

The face of American aid changed after the Second World War. The Marshall Plan in Europe pointed the way toward development through economic assistance. Public Law 480 took effect during the Eisenhower administration and set the pattern for U.S. food relief for the next three decades. The Kennedy years saw the birth of the Peace Corps and the U.S. Agency for International Development. The law that gave us U.S. AID (the acronym was not accidental) again set the pattern for future economic assistance. No longer was U.S. economic aid to be limited to disaster relief or famine relief; it was meant to be a tool of foreign policy, to promote economic growth, encourage free enterprise and democracy, and to serve as a weapon in the growing arsenal fighting the encroachment of Communism around the globe.

But foreign aid has never had a strong domestic constituency. Public opinion polls over the years have shown broad but shallow support for foreign economic assistance. According to one long-time observer of foreign assistance programs, "the passage of U.S. AID's enabling legislation, the Foreign Assistance Act of 1961, under the charismatic leadership of President Kennedy, marks the last time an administration has successfully mobilized broad support for aid."[1] Public attitudes toward aid are ambivalent, to say the least, and this ambivalence eventually works its way into the authorizing and defining legislation for AID and other agencies. A 1987 poll sponsored by the Overseas Development Council and InterAction found that 89 percent of Americans believe "wherever people are hungry or poor, we ought to do what we can to help them." However, the same poll showed that 84 percent agree with the statement that "we need to solve our own poverty problems in the United States before we turn attention to other countries." While a slight majority of Americans support foreign aid, about the same number believe "we should give the Third World countries less aid and leave them alone" and 62 percent fear that "aid programs get us too mixed up with other countries' affairs."[2]

These varied goals and attitudes have inevitably led to disagreements about the shape of economic aid. The Korry Report of 1966, written by the then-U.S. ambassador to Ethiopia at the urging of Senator William Fulbright, the powerful chairman of the Senate Foreign Relations Committee, recommended that AID assistance should be directed to a few countries where it could do the most good, so that within a few years after that report, the number of African countries receiving AID help fell from thirty-five to ten. Yet two decades later, with a different emphasis on the foreign policy goals of AID, the number of countries again reached thirty-five.[3]

During the 1970s, AID's mission was redefined by "New Directions" legislation that, among other things, mandated that AID work directly with poor people in developing countries. The "New Directions" amendments also restructured the AID budget, which from 1961 to 1973 had been fairly flexible and divided into just two categories, development loans and technical assistance. After 1973, AID's budget had to be divided into "functional" categories.[4] (Problems associated with congressional oversight of functional budgeting will be discussed in Chapter Two.)

The Purposes of U.S. Economic Aid

The goals of U.S. economic aid are interrelated and sometimes contradictory. Critics of foreign assistance programs often cite the "hopeless patchwork" of mandates assigned to AID by Congress and the executive branch. Current AID policy is to scale down its efforts. When Mark L. Edelman was sworn in as deputy director of the agency in July 1989, he said: "There are too many worthy causes to take up, too many people to help. We must say no to some if we are to successfully tackle others. . . . We cannot continue under the constant pressure to be all things to all people, while remaining responsible guardians of American tax dollars."[5] Despite the pressures applied to them and the considerable overlap among program goals, it may be useful to examine the major goals of U.S. aid policy separately.

First, *to alleviate hunger and poverty:* This goal is so fundamental that it may need no explanation. A few points should be noted, however. Famine relief and disaster relief usually, but not always, transcend ideological or political issues. When the Soviet Union suffered a devastating earthquake in Armenia just before Christmas 1988, the United States was among the first countries to send aid. In the mid-1980s, the government-induced famine in Ethiopia reached such unimaginable proportions that the U.S. government and individual Americans and their philanthropic associations could hardly stand by without lending a hand. Only later, when it became clear that the Derg, Ethiopia's ruling Leninist junta, had fashioned the widespread hunger for its own purposes, did the U.S. and other Western governments begin to withhold bilateral economic assistance.[6]

In Africa as a whole, food has been a major portion of the U.S. AID program for the continent. In 1985, for example, AID directed about one billion dollars to almost three dozen countries, not including a number of emergency relief projects that were not part of the agency's appropriated budget for the year.[7] AID's congressional budget request for fiscal year 1990 notes that:

> emergency food assistance will continue to be one of A.I.D.'s points of intervention for actually coping with famine, but A.I.D. will focus increasingly on preparedness by: developing famine early warning networks in countries particularly prone to drought . . . ; fostering the growth of food needs assessment capacity; supporting grass-roots PVO [Private Voluntary Organization] activities . . . ; and generally encouraging the growth of public and private institutions which can respond.[8]

The total request for PL480 funds for 1990 is approximately $172 million, compared to $174 million (estimated) for 1989 and $288 million spent in 1988.[9]

A second goal of U.S. development aid is *to encourage the growth of free enterprise.* For much of the first twenty or so years of AID's existence, this goal underlay its work but was not an explicitly motivating goal. In the past decade, however, especially with pressures being put on Third World countries by the World Bank and the International Monetary Fund to reform their economic systems as a condition for loans, AID has adjusted its programs to assist small-scale and medium-size private businesses in Africa. In 1981, AID launched its Private Enterprise Initiative at the direction of President Ronald Reagan, who said at the time:

> The societies that have achieved the most spectacular, broad-based economic progress in the shortest period of time are not the tightly-controlled, nor necessarily the biggest in size, nor the wealthiest in natural resources. No, what unites them is their willingness to believe in the magic of the marketplace.[10]

To be sure, the market-oriented approach has met opposition both at home and in the host countries. At home, bureaucrats and Capitol Hill policymakers maintained a "macroeconomic" perspective that served, essentially, as blinders against the "microeconomic" policies necessary to encourage free enterprise. This resistance is eroding, however, and with the publication of the Woods Report in early 1989 (*Development and the National Interest: U.S. Economic Assistance into the 21st Century*, commissioned by the late Alan Woods, administrator of the Agency for International Development), most policymakers in both the executive and legislative branches agreed that it best served U.S. interests and the interests of developing nations to support and assist the growth of private enterprise.

One reason for supporting private enterprise is that it may help *promote democracy*, the third goal of U.S. economic assistance. Third World — and especially African — political leaders are often skeptical about, if not actually hostile, toward free enterprise. Despite growing historical evidence to the contrary, African elites believe that capitalism was imposed on their countries by foreigners — first colonial masters and now multilateral lending institutions. Moreover, African political leaders believe that any dilution of centralized power works against them. Private entrepreneurs, no matter how small-scale, are an effective wedge against total state control of society. The business community forms a mediating structure, a counterweight to government power. In league with churches, labor unions, and a free press, merchants and manufacturers can destroy totalitarian or pseudo-totalitarian rulers.

This, of course, is the promise Western elites see in *perestroika*, Mikhail Gorbachev's plan of economic restructuring in the Soviet Union. The Bush administration has promised a small amount of economic aid to Poland and Hungary to help the growth of private enterprise there. American academics are praising Gorbachev — and until the Tiananmen Square massacre praised China's Deng Xiaoping — for their attempts to liberalize Marxist economies along Western lines. Yet this liberalization has been much more limited than many would like to believe; in fact, it can be argued — as Zbigniew Brzezinski, Charles Fairbanks, and others have — that "*glasnost, perestroika,* and 'democraticization' were policies Gorbachev adopted both to consolidate power and to save the Communist system *and* Soviet military domination" of its satellite states.[11] Still, the reason the Reagan and Bush administrations have been so optimistic is that genuine economic liberalization can do little else but weaken the totalitarian control of the Communist party. This brings us to the fourth goal of U.S. economic assistance in the Third World: *to discourage the spread of Communism.* Communist economic and political systems promise little to the poor and hungry people of Africa, Asia, and Latin America. Yet intellectuals on those continents have bought into Marxist analysis simply because they believed no alternative was forthcoming from the West. Moreover, economic liberalism did not offer Third World elites the raw power of Marxism-Leninism with its concentrated monopoly of political and economic decision making.

For far too long the United States did not take advantage of free enterprise and its proven record of productivity as a weapon in its arsenal of democracy. That has changed.

In 1982, Ronald Reagan, in a speech before the British Parliament, called for an all-out effort to spread democracy around the world. One result of that call was the National Endowment for Democracy, a federally-funded private foundation that uses its money to support democratic ideals and movements in the Third World and the Communist bloc. One of its channels is the Center for International Private Enterprise (CIPE), a project of the U.S. Chamber of Commerce. CIPE is in the forefront of encouraging small business development in the Third World, and much of what it does could serve as a model for future development assistance programs.

Standards to Measure Success

Whether U.S. economic development aid has been successful depends in large part on the yardstick used to measure it. A criticism, not only of U.S. AID but also of multilateral organizations such as the World Bank and the IMF, is that bureaucratic standards of success differ significantly from political or even purely economic standards. A World Bank manager, for instance, measures the success of the program she manages by the amount of resources poured into it. Modest results from the project satisfy her. An AID bureaucrat might be pleased with concrete results, with hardware such as a dam or irrigation system, rather than with the intangible (and thus immeasurable) results of an improved quality of life for the people AID ostensibly assists. It is, after all, easier to point to a dam when questioned by Congress than it is to say that villagers in certain parts of Africa are more content today than they were yesterday. What many international aid experts and officials fail to acknowledge is that "actual human welfare can be independent of official government activity."[12] These intangibles deserve more attention.

With the Woods Report, however, AID's success will depend much more on encouraging widespread, self-sustaining prosperity and supporting the growth of free enterprise, rather than simply aiming for large-scale projects that are easy to claim as successful. AID has made a preliminary effort to develop a "policy matrix" called an "Economic Opportunity Index," designed to show the impact of policies meant to promote individual opportunity and economic competition. Some of the factors of the Economic Opportunity Index are:

- property rights including broad-based and reliable land tenure arrangements, the level of official corruption, and the effectiveness of legal remedies to enforce contracts

- the consistency and credibility of past government policy and regulations, including the ability to adjust to external shocks

- credit and monetary policy: the extent of directed credit, and whether deposit rates are higher than inflation

- taxation: whether there are preferences to inefficient industries, and the incentive effects of marginal tax rates

- other controls over markets for food, shelter, and labor

- foreign exchange controls and the size of black markets[13]

Similar standards were adopted by the U.S. Senate in an amendment to the Foreign Assistance Act of 1989 submitted by Senator Connie Mack (R-Florida), which mandates that AID administer an "Index of Economic Freedom" when creating its programs. There are some who argue that this legislation is a fine idea but that AID will never be able to use it effectively. One reason is a bureaucratic "groupthink" resistance to any such new mandate; another is that AID simply lacks the resources to carry out what the "index" requires.[14]

Enhancing the Standards

While these standards are a good place to start, by themselves they cannot fully promote prosperity and freedom in underdeveloped African countries. They are too broadly drawn, utopian, and vague. The Index of Economic Freedom is to some extent merely a mirror-image of the Global Poverty Reduction Act, which was added as an amendment to the Foreign Assistance Act in the House of Representatives at about the same time that Senator Mack introduced the Index of Economic Freedom in the Senate. The Global Poverty Reduction Act was designed by a grassroots public interest lobby called Results. It requires AID and other agencies to demonstrate the effectiveness of foreign assistance programs by measuring the under-five-years-old mortality rate, the literacy rate among females, and "absolute" poverty. The GPRA has been criticized by veteran diplomat William Middendorf as "simply a rehash of old, shopworn ideas which sensible people in Washington now want to discard."[15] Ambassador Middendorf went on to note that the GPRA attacks the symptoms, not the causes of poverty, turning U.S. foreign assistance programs into "welfare agents to the Third World."

As a substitute for the social-welfare solution proposed by Results — which said that U.S. foreign aid policies should be directed toward "increasing opportunities for the poor, rather than reflecting, or directed toward, overall economic growth" — Ambassador Middendorf correctly suggested that U.S. policy should be redirected toward "greater growth in the poorest sectors of the countries in which we have programs." He further stated that, "Broad-based growth is the precondition for sustained solutions to all those symptoms of poverty" and also to ecological problems of concern to environmentalists.[16]

In order for such a redirection of effort to work, however, U.S. AID needs to redefine its terms. It needs to get down to specifics. U.S. policy must seek success in four separate but interrelated categories: (1) grassroots economic reform, working through the informal sector and providing financial, legal, and moral support for small businesses that face obstacles erected by the state; (2) broad deregulation, including streamlining or eliminating licensing requirements for small and micro-businesses; (3) privatization of large, state-owned enterprises; and (4) the contraction of the state, including the revising of legal codes to protect private property and encourage individual initiative.

AID is uniquely well-placed to pursue this line of development. In the first place, our allies in the foreign assistance business, such as the European Community and Japan, have not been motivated to encourage private enterprise development. According to Richard Bissell, these donors (1) are "not oriented toward the private sector," (2) have small field missions and lack the resources to work with the private sector, and (3) have limited their experience to working through cooperatives (large numbers of small farmers, for example, working together) rather than encouraging individual small entrepreneurs. As a result, U.S. AID is just about the only international development agency with a legislative mandate to encourage free enterprise in the sense discussed here.[17] Furthermore, the multilateral development and lending institutions — the World Bank and the IMF — lack legal sanction to pursue this course. An AID Africa Bureau official noted at a Center for International Private Enterprise conference in February 1989 that despite their interest in structural adjustment and economic sectoral reform, the World Bank and IMF are "institutionally prohibited from doing certain things," that they lack a charter "to directly intervene" in areas like "social/legal systems, market operations, things that get into the structure of the country and are often inherently political." Because the World Bank and IMF have tied hands, he said, the "bilateral donors are going to have to play more of a role."[18]

Methodology and Purpose

To explore these issues more deeply, we have chosen to look at seven African countries and U.S. AID programs in those countries. In each case, we were most interested in whether AID was encouraging small-scale private enterprise and, if so, what effect that encouragement had on the larger economy. Each case study gives a broad overview of political and economic developments in that country over the past decade or so, including general information about population, major exports, industries, rates of economic growth or decline, and significant World Bank or IMF programs in the country. Chapter One provides an even broader overview of the economic situation on the African continent as of 1989, looking at economic performance since the advent of World Bank-initiated structural adjustment and prospects for future reform. Chapter Two looks at how the U.S. Agency for International Development is organized and examine its shortcomings. This will be followed by case studies of Botswana, Ivory Coast, Ghana, Kenya, Senegal, South Africa, and Swaziland. It should be noted that because of the difficulties in obtaining accurate and complete information about economic conditions in African countries, some chapters will be lengthier and, frankly, more interesting, than others. (The problem of data-gathering will also be discussed in Chapter One.)

The purpose of this study should be stated simply and clearly at the outset. It is meant to promote the growth of free enterprise around the globe and to encourage the spread of democratic capitalism with all that that term entails: as defined by Michael Novak, systems of democratic capitalism consist of "a predominantly market economy; a polity respectful of the rights of the individual to life, liberty, and the pursuit of happiness; and a system of cultural institutions moved by ideals of liberty and justice for all."[19] In the short term, it is hoped that this study will influence future American policy, and policies of other Western countries, so that foreign assistance programs can become more rational, more practical, and more oriented toward encouraging growth and prosperity through people rather than governments.

Liberal democracy is acquiring more credibility around the world every day. In a widely discussed article, titled "The End of History?" and published in the *National Interest*,[20] U.S. State Department official Francis Fukuyama asserted that we have come to the end of the cycle of history in which ideologies confront each other for control of the world. The gist of his argument is that totalitarian ideologies have lost the struggle for world dominance. Fascism was defeated in World War II and Communism was defeated by the Cold War. More importantly, however, the *idea* of liberal democracy — in Novak's term, democratic capitalism — has come to predominate. Political elites in Communist states, socialist states, and the Third World have lost the fervor with which they formerly fought for the triumph of their ideologies. They have thrown in the towel to the extent that in Poland, opposition parties led by the Solidarity trade-union movement have effective control of the *Sejm* (parliament) and that in Hungary, a stock exchange is being established. The Berlin Wall has collapsed under the weight of the cultural contradictions of Communism, and in Czechoslovakia the Prague Spring seems finally to have triumphed.

Still, there is no room for complacency. Genuine reform will be slow in coming and will bring in its path uncertainty, instability, painful adjustment, and even — as in Romania—widespread violence. As Eric Chenoweth, editor of the journal *Uncaptive Minds*, put it, "We are witnessing the decline of this century's most dangerous experiment to create a Communist civilization. It will not just fade away; it will take a very long time to decline; at each stage, the Communist leadership will take advantage of economic, political, and perhaps military resources to maintain its power."[21]   Free-market oriented economic reforms and access to Western education led inexorably to the massacre of Chinese students in Tiananmen Square on June 4, 1989, because the demands for more freedom became an unavoidable threat to the political monopoly enjoyed by the Chinese Communist Party. There may perhaps be nothing so dangerous as a totalitarian system in the paroxysms of death. Hunters know that a fatally wounded predator can be the most dangerous of beasts.

Notes to Introduction:

[1]Allan Hoben, "USAID: Organizational and Institutional Issues and Effectiveness," in Robert J. Berg and David F. Gordon, eds., *Cooperation for International Development: The United States and the Third World in the 1990s* (Boulder, Colo.: Lynne Rienner Publishers, 1989), p. 257.

[2]John Maxwell Hamilton, "Development Cooperation: Creating a Public Commitment," in Robert J. Berg and David F. Gordon, eds., *Cooperation for International Development: The United States and the Third World in the 1990s* (Boulder, Colo.: Lynne Rienner Publishers, 1989), p. 213.

[3]Carl K. Eicher, "Strategic Issues in Combating Hunger and Poverty in Africa," in Robert J. Berg and Jennifer Seymour Whitaker, *Strategies for African Development* (Berkeley, Calif.: University of California Press, 1986), p. 266.

[4]Theodor W. Galdi, "Development Assistance Policy: A Historical Overview," in *Background Materials on Foreign Assistance*, Report of the Task Force on Foreign Assistance to the Committee on Foreign Affairs, U.S. House of Representatives, February 1989, pp. 250-51.

[5]"For the Record," *The Washington Post*, July 28, 1989, p. A24.

[6]See Myles Harris, *Breakfast in Hell: A Doctor's Experiences of the Ethiopian Famine* (London: Picador, 1986).

[7] Eicher, "Strategic Issues in Combating Hunger and Poverty," p. 266.

[8] Agency for International Development, *Congressional Presentation Fiscal Year 1990, Annex I, Africa*, p. 38.

[9] Ibid., p. 26.

[10]Cited in *Economic Growth and the Third World: A Report on the AID Private Enterprise Initiative* (Washington: Agency for International Development, 1987), p. 4.

[11]Eric Chenoweth, "Communism in Decline," letter, *Commentary*, December 1989, p. 15.

[12]Interview with Richard Bissell, assistant administrator for program and policy development, U.S. Agency for International Development, June 29, 1989.

[13] U.S. Agency for International Development, *Development and the National Interest: U.S. Economic Assistance into the 21st Century* (Washington: U.S. AID, 1989), p. 52.

[14]Interview with John Sullivan, director of congressional and public affairs, Center for International Private Enterprise, July 7, 1989.

[15]William Middendorf, "Poverty Reduction Mischief," *The Washington Times*, June 27, 1989, p. F1.

[16]Ibid., p. F4.

[17]Interview with Richard Bissell, June 29, 1989.

[18]Unpublished transcript, conference on "Market-Oriented Paths to Economic Growth: Lessons of the 1980s," break-out session on Sub-Saharan Africa, Center for International Private Enterprise, Washington, D.C., February 15, 1989, pp. 83-84.

[19]Michael Novak, *The Spirit of Democratic Capitalism* (New York: Simon and Schuster, 1982), p. 14.

[20]Francis Fukuyama, "The End of History?," *The National Interest* 16, Summer 1989, pp. 3-18, with responses by Allan Bloom, Pierre Hassner, Gertrude Himmelfarb, Irving Kristol, Daniel Patrick Moynihan, and Stephen Sestanovich, pp. 19-35.

[21]Chenoweth, "Communism in Decline," p. 17.

1

An Overview:
Economic Conditions and
Development Policy
in Sub-Saharan Africa

A remarkable rhetorical consensus has emerged on the question of U.S. economic aid in the Third World. After years of looking at development aid through macroeconomic spectacles only as some gigantic, worldwide welfare program, policymakers are finally beginning to recognize the importance of wealth creation through individual initiative. The concrete benefits of capitalism have finally been shown to outweigh its theoretical disadvantages. At the Senate hearings that preceded his confirmation as Secretary of State, James A. Baker, III, told the Foreign Relations Committee:

> Free markets and private initiative are the new watchwords of economic development — because these concepts work in practice. Classic socialism and variants of government-controlled economies have been discredited. The nations of the Pacific Rim in particular have shown that the free enterprise model works astonishingly well for developing economies, not just mature economies.[1]

In 1989 alone, two reports — *Development and the National Interest*, also called the Woods Report, named after the late administrator of the Agency for International Development, and *Report on the Task Force on Foreign Assistance*, also called the Hamilton Report, named for the co-chairman of an ad hoc subcommittee of the House Foreign Affairs committee — produced independently of each other, read similarly in their conclusions. Mark L. Edelman, deputy administrator of U.S. AID, summed up the new consensus well in a speech at his swearing-in ceremony in July 1989: "The role of government is to promote optio ns, not impose solutions. Governments will not produce development any more than welfare will." Most of the world's people, he said, "are pretty good at determining what is best for them — if they are given the tools and freedom to make a choice. . . . AID must be an agency for growth, for opportunity, for individual choice."[2]

This consensus did not emerge overnight. Credit must be given to those who worked hard in the conservative and classical liberal think tanks that lent advice and expertise to the Reagan and Bush administrations. But it is not in American intellectual circles alone that have seen the triumph of free enterprise. In Europe, the example of Margaret Thatcher's program of privatization has been a bright beacon. And by studying the slums of Peru, economist Hernando de Soto produced an exhaustive study, *The Other Path: The Invisible Revolution in the Third World*, which was a best-seller in the author's native Latin America. Since its publication in the United States in early 1989, it has had the entire foreign policy community buzzing with its implications.

What de Soto's work has shown is the pervasiveness of the "informal sector" in Third World economies. The informal sector — also known as the second sector, the informal economy, the gray market, the black market, the underground economy — is that part of the economy which exists apart from the official, formal sector. That is, those who work in the informal sector — street hawkers, taxi drivers, clothing manufacturers, shoe-shine operators — do so without the benefit of government sanction or license. This means, too, that they have no protection for their businesses: no right to enforce contracts in court, no way to buy insurance, no means to keep a bank account or establish credit, no ability to apply to the government for easements or rights-of-way on public property. In other words, informal sector businesses must operate at great risk with marginal profitability. Yet despite all these disadvantages they manage to produce housing, opportunity, and wealth without which the total economies of these countries would collapse.

How does the informal sector come about? Adam Smith himself noted in *The Wealth of Nations* that the urge of every individual to better himself economically "is so powerful a principle, that it is alone and without any assistance, not only capable of carrying on the society to health and prosperity, but of surmounting a hundred impertinent obstructions with which the folly of human laws too often encumbers its operations."[3] In the Third World, overregulation stems from the fear governments have of the private sector. They have created rules and regulations, mountains of red tape, in the belief that they can better control their economies and thus the political life of their societies. Yet the economic impulse is so pervasive and so strong in individuals that the informal sector arises and even thrives despite all efforts of governments to subdue it. John Maynard Keynes recognized this more than two generations ago in his classic essay, *The End of Laissez-Faire*:

> Above all, the ineptitude of public administrators strongly prejudiced the practical man in favor of *laissez-faire* — a sentiment which has by no means disappeared. Almost everything which the state did in the 18th century in excess of its minimum functions was, or seemed, injurious or unsuccessful.[4]

Adds Professor Deepak Lal of University College, London: "Anyone familiar with the actual administration and implementation of policies in very many Third World countries, and not blinkered by the *Dirigiste Dogma*, should find that oft-neglected work, *The Wealth of Nations*, both so relevant and so modern."[5] Professor Lal notes that there is a large body of empirical evidence that shows "that uneducated peasants act economically as producers and consumers. They respond to changes in relative prices much as neo-classical economic theory predicts." Adam Smith's "Economic Principle," he writes, "is not unrealistic in the Third World."[6]

Black Market or Second Economy?

The impulse of the Economic Principle channels the energies of many small entrepreneurs into what government authorities in Africa call the "black market." The term "black market" brings to mind all sorts of sinister images. In the United States, the black market is where stolen goods or illicit drugs are bought and sold. During the Second World War, the black market dealt in hard-to-find consumer goods and ration tickets. Who can forget the haunting images in *Casablanca* of refugees from Nazi-ruled Europe who sold anything and did anything to acquire visas to freedom?

Any visitor to the Soviet Union, for instance, can tell you of the brash young people who buy dollars and sell rubles to American tourists, often in broad daylight on Red Square, boldly defying Soviet laws that promise harsh penalties to those who trade currency outside the official exchange bureaus.[7]

In unfree countries, the black market is more properly termed the "parallel market" or "second economy," where individuals can engage in their inalienable right to seek economic betterment despite the best efforts of the state to control the economy. Except in the case of truly illicit business dealings — such as trade in drugs or armaments or slaves — this study will use the term "informal sector" to describe black market activities as well as small, technically illegal manufacturing activities, technically illegal homebuilding on undeveloped government land ("squatting"), and the operation of technically illegal transport systems.

Since independence from colonial rule, Third World governments have tried hard to impose restrictions on trade. In these countries, nationalization of basic industries has been the rule, and mountains of red tape stand in the way of any enterprising person who wants to start a business, however small. In Africa, the parallel market can amount to 50 percent of the "official" economy, skewing the figures used to determine gross national product, national budgets, and development aid from the industrialized countries.

The June 1989 issue of the magazine *African Business*[8] explored this topic in some depth. African countries have persistent shortages of consumer goods — not just luxury items, but basics like soap, corn meal, and cooking oil. To combat this scarcity — usually caused by unwarranted government intervention in the economy through price-fixing and forced collectivization of agriculture — individual entrepreneurs turn to smuggling and illegal trade. And they are wildly successful.

In Ghana, for instance, even the government-run foreign exchange offices must rely on the illegal currency traders to keep their shops afloat. Shortages of hard currency (dollars, francs, marks, yen) in the official "forex" bureaus are made up when Ghanaian officials buy what they need from the enterprising traders on the street.

In Zaire, too, officially sanctioned businesses could not survive if it were not for the parallel market. In the southern city of Lubumbashi, a prominent businesswoman, Mujinga Tshibangu, told *African Business*, "These people are a major source of our business. We couldn't do without them."[9] The report notes the contrast between the government's view of the black marketeer and that of struggling businessmen (and women):

> The black marketeer who makes annual appearances as the villain in [parliamentary] budget speeches is depicted as a money-grubbing, dishonorable traitor. Tshibangu's black marketeer is first and foremost a businessman — a wholesaler whom she knows she can count on to keep her regularly supplied with merchandise.[10]

Despite the pervasive poverty throughout the African continent, there are relative differences between countries. Zimbabwe, for instance, is a consumers' and workers' paradise (despite the pro-Marxist regime of Robert Mugabe) compared to neighboring Zambia, where the economic policies of President Kenneth Kaunda have caused stagnation and deterioration. Thus, in dark of night, Zambians cross the border to the Zimbabwean tourist resort of Victoria Falls to bring back inexpensive sugar, bread, flour, margarine, soap, rice, and soft drinks (especially Coca-Cola, which in some African countries is prized more than gold). The smugglers either keep these goods for their own use or sell them to less enterprising countrymen.

Estimates of the size of the informal sector vary from country to country and according to who is doing the counting. Hernando de Soto asserts the informal sector in his native Peru accounts for nearly 40 percent of gross domestic product (GDP).[11] Argentinian economist Marcos Victorica argues that in his country, the informal economy amounts to 60 percent of gross national product (GNP).[12] In the urban areas of Kenya, according to that country's ministry of planning and national development, the informal sector employs about 40 percent of the work force.[13] Nevertheless, Brazilian economist Eliana A. Cardoso charges that such figures rest on "statistical fragility" that "invalidates [their] usefulness for economic evaluation and sends the wrong signals to policymakers."[14]

Why is the informal sector so big? University of Wisconsin Professor Edgar Feige explains that one of the fundamental problems of development is the inability of capital-intensive formal sector firms to provide jobs for the large labor supply that migrates to urban areas from the countryside, a migration that is often accelerated by government price-fixing that makes farming unprofitable and life in rural areas untenable. As such, "the existence and growth of the informal economy represents a prime *symptom* of the development problem — a large pool of the underemployed, or 'working poor.'"[15] John Sullivan of the Center for International Private Enterprise agrees, noting that the existence of a large informal sector is symptomatic of a diseased economy. The informal sector, he says, is a bad thing. Its existence tells us that the formal sector — that part of the economy approved by the government — is sclerotic, corrupt, inefficient. The informal sector must operate under tremendous disadvantages: its participants have no access to credit (except through loan sharks), cannot enforce contracts because they have no access to the courts, cannot take advantage of government services, have no protection against market fluctuations or police harassment, and — for all these reasons — cannot expand beyond the microlevel.[16]

Dealing with the Data Problem

The existence of a large informal sector and black markets creates real problems for governments and for international development agencies. Richard Bissell, assistant administrator for program and policy coordination at U.S. AID, points out that the informal sector, which is so active in Third World countries, creates a sort of "psychic dissonance" for government planners and development agencies. Its existence generates skewed figures at the macroeconomic level; there is no way to accurately judge employment, nutrition, and other factors as long as the informal sector is barred from the formal economy.[17] This troubling characteristic compounds the more mundane problems in data collection that make development planning so difficult. The World Bank admits to a "paucity" of socioeconomic data in most African countries; information on income distribution, consumption patterns, and the evolution of household incomes is especially hard to come by.[18] The United Nations lists only seven African countries with essentially complete systems of compiling information such as mortality statistics; none of these seven countries are part of the Sub-Saharan region. Until the mid-1970s, more than a decade after independence, most Sub-Saharan countries had not yet done a complete census.[19] Moreover, far beyond these logistical and pragmatic troubles, there is the fundamental problem that must be faced: the entire theory of development assistance, as it is currently understood, is flawed.

The Poverty of 'Development Economics'

To understand the current sad state of economic development in Sub-Saharan Africa, one must go back to the early independence period. Most African countries became independent of their colonial rulers in 1960 and shortly thereafter. At first, there was considerable hope that economic growth would continue at the same rate as it had in the late colonial era. Conventional economic views had it that with the influx of Western development aid, African countries would be able to sustain an export-led economic growth rate of 5 percent or more.

Unfortunately, for both political and economic reasons, African governments adopted *dirigiste*, or statist, economic policies whose effect was to stifle growth. As Indian economist Deepak Lal put it in his aptly-titled book, *The Poverty of "Development Economics,"* "The most serious current distortions in many developing countries are not those flowing from the inevitable imperfections of a market economy but the policy-induced, and thus far from inevitable, distortions created by irrational *dirigisme.*"[20] Many of these statist policies were adopted wholesale and essentially unchanged from the colonial governments; Britain, for instance, adopted monopoly marketing boards for agricultural commodities in its West African colonies during the Second World War and simply grew too comfortable with them to abolish the boards when the wartime emergency was over. Despite the fact that these monopolies constrained agricultural development, independent African states retained them — and, in many cases, expanded them — as part of their colonial patrimony.[21] In other words, current poverty in Third World countries — and, as we shall see, especially in Africa — is the result of conscious policy decisions by ruling elites, often aided by development economists trained in the West or employed by Western-financed development agencies who quite readily discarded the classical and orthodox economics in the tradition of Adam Smith, David Ricardo, and even John Maynard Keynes in favor of dicier theories and practices.

A large part of this prejudice toward interventionism and state-oriented economic planning arose from a fundamental distrust of the common people to perform economically. Development economists simply felt that illiterate masses of the Third World were unprepared to take on the tasks necessary for economic growth, conveniently ignoring the fact that economic growth in the First World — Western Europe, Britain, and North America — was secured in the first place by largely uneducated "masses" who were the human engine of the industrial revolution. The paternalism has often been contempt — masked with the terminology of scientific analysis. As one critic of development economics has explained:

> If one were to tell the politicians of the underdeveloped countries that their people are lazy, stupid, lacking in initiative and adaptability, one would be branded as an enemy; but if one were to rephrase these prejudices in another way and say that the people lack entrepreneurial capacity, one would be welcomed for giving "scientific" support for economic planning.[22]

It is no accident that in this context a rebellion of sorts has taken place in the development field. The Woods Report and the Hamilton Report are but two symbols of the rebellion, as is de Soto's *The Other Path.*

Development Aid — A 'Shambles'

Perhaps the most trenchant and unconventional critique of orthodox development economics is found in Jane Jacobs widely-discussed 1984 book, *Cities and the Wealth of Nations.* In it, Jacobs tackles head-on the field of macroeconomics and the development policies that flow from it, calling the whole field "a shambles." Charging that as a science, development economics has been overindulged, Jacobs asserts that "never have experiments left in their wakes more wreckage, unpleasant surprises, blasted hopes, and confusion, to the point that the question seriously arises whether the wreckage is reparable; if it is, certainly not with more of the same."[23]

Criticism of development assistance does not come just from Westerners who are dissatisfied with its results. Recipients of the aid complain, too. For instance, the minister of health for Swaziland, Fanny Friedman, addressed the 1989

Conference of the National Council for International Health in Arlington, Virginia, in these words:

> The word aid, as in foreign aid, is a misnomer. Many donor agencies and countries have policies which lead to the development of dependence rather than dependence. . . . . Even when the intent is good, such policies can result in uneven development and lack of sustainability, often ending in alienation, distrust between various sectors in the country and/or between host country and donor. Such situations may arise, for example, when local programs have to give up resources in favor of the donor's programs.[24]

Like others who have analyzed the history of development aid, Jacobs notes that the impulse to send aid to underdeveloped countries was electrified by the success of the Marshall Plan in post-war Western Europe. The problem, of course, is that Marshall Plan aid was intended to repair fully developed but war-damaged economies, not transform embryonic economies *ex nihilo*. "The healing of organisms —" she says, "including the organisms known as economies — is not at all the same as the metamorphosis of organisms, the conversion of them into something different."[25] Since the growing development industry of the 1950s and 1960s insisted on calling its projects "mini-Marshall Plans" and the like, disappointment was inevitable — and came at a high price. One estimate is that in the thirty years ending in 1986, the West transferred about $1.6 trillion to the Third World — an amount equal to the total worth of all industrial stock traded on the New York Stock Exchange, and double the value of the entire U.S. agricultural sector.[26]

The failure of the development economists stemmed from their definition of development. They saw poverty as an obstacle to be overcome. They used military rhetoric to define development as a single-minded goal that can be reached by strategies, long-term planning, and setting targets. The unstated assumption was that "economic life can be conquered, mobilized, bullied, as indeed it can be when it is directed toward warfare, but not when it directs itself to development and expansion."[27] Moreover, as Michael Novak has often pointed out, development economists are forever seeking the "causes of poverty." Poverty, across all cultures and for most of human history, is mankind's normal state. What needs to be explored are the causes of wealth. Fortunately, that project was set off on a good start by Adam Smith in 1776.

The key, argues Jacobs, is that by its very nature, "successful economic development has to be open-ended rather than goal-oriented, and has to make itself up expediently and empirically as it goes along."[28] Jacobs defines economic development "as a process of continually improvising in a context that makes injecting improvisations into everyday life feasible," amplifying this definition with the concept of "drift": development entails "unprecedented kinds of work that carry unprecedented problems, [which drift into] improvised solutions, which carry further unprecedented work carrying unprecedented problems. . ."[29]

Small-scale economic actors in the Third World can be remarkably flexible in this fashion. Precisely because of the precariousness of their situation (most often in the unprotected, informal sector), peasants and micro-entrepreneurs respond well to the price mechanism. Deepak Lal argues that "unlike in richer countries, economic agents in poor ones will have few 'reserves' to fall back upon and will thus have to adjust speedily to a change in their economic environment by swiftly altering the terms on which they are willing to exchange economic commodities." In developed economies, protected by large savings or the safety net of the welfare state, economic actors "can postpone the required price adjustments in a changing economic environment."[30]

It seems clear from this analysis that the informal sector — which, after all, existed and grew in the pre-modern era in Western countries even during the age of mercantilism — is the most effective engine of economic growth. The informal sector alone — unencumbered by the conservatism and officiousness of bureaucracies and   political elites, ready to adjust to changing conditions, and willing to risk arrest and prosecution in order to achieve economic success — can create the conditions for growth even in the poorest of countries.

Political and Legal Considerations

In *The Other Path*, Hernando de Soto demonstrates the negative effect of overregulation and the absence of legal protections for property and enterprise. In painstaking detail, de Soto shows how difficult it was to establish a textile factory in Peru — it took almost 300 days to apply for permits, get approvals, and generally complete the paperwork to establish a tiny business. In New York City, the same bureaucratic procedures took a few hours. Bypassing the paperwork altogether allowed the business to be up and running within a matter of a few days. And so it is throughout the Third World, especially in Africa.

Economic change does not take place in a cultural or social vacuum. Neither does the informal sector exist fully apart from the formal sector. Formal-sector industries buy raw materials and products from informal counterparts; workers in formal-sector factories buy their lunches from informal-sector street vendors; informal-sector businesses, in turn, get finished goods to sell from formal-sector manufacturers and wholesalers. Despite the herculean efforts of small-scale entrepreneurs in the informal sector, their further expansion into national and world markets is impeded by political and legal systems that for various reasons prefer regulation to freedom. There must be an effort to reform these systems before economic success can be assured.

However, stimulating the growth of the informal sector can serve a secondary function; namely, to prod the state to reform itself. Elie Kedourie, the distinguished political scientist from the University of London, argues that:

> even if informal economic activity must remain hobbled and crippled and unable to bring full benefits either to those who engage in it or to society at large, such activity . . . is nevertheless

greatly to be preferred to its absence. . . . If those who engage in informal activity can organize themselves, they can bring pressure and influence to bear on power-holders and those who seek to replace them.[31]

Philip Nicolaides, managing director of the Foundation for Africa's Future, provides one example. "The rise of SABTA (the Southern African Black Taxi Association," he writes:

> provides a striking case history of the power of the informal sector. Ten years ago, it was just a handful of minivan owners using pay phones and getting together at gas stations to work out routes to help black people — long neglected by state-subsidized transit operations — to get to work. Today SABTA has an owner-membership of 48,000, employs some 120,000 people directly, and has indirectly created perhaps 300,000 new jobs. Its members transport more than a million people to and from their jobs every day.

> SABTA's president recalls the time not many years ago when he was snubbed and slighted by petty bureaucrats. The government contemplated regulations that would have stifled SABTA's growth. Today things are different. Today he is called in to consult with cabinet officers and even the state president — a dramatic illustration of how economic power can translate into political power.[32]

What are the basic political and legal conditions that must be met before the power of the informal sector can be fully felt? Fundamentally, there must be a constitutional system of government that is not subject to arbitrary and capricious actions on the part of office-holders. This provides the minimum of political and economic security necessary for any entrepreneur to believe that he will gain future benefits from his current labors and risks. Unfortunately, most

Third World countries lack stable constitutional regimes. In Africa, only a handful of countries have not been subject to military coups since independence; not so coincidentally, those with the most stable governments — Botswana, Ivory Coast, Kenya, Senegal, and South Africa — are also those that show the most sustained economic growth over the past quarter century. (Tanzania, which also has had an unusually stable post-independence regime, has had a steadily deteriorating economy — often on the brink of collapse —due to wrongheaded government policies instituted by Julius Nyerere, father of "African Socialism."[33] This despite the fact that Tanzania is "the most aided country in all of Africa."[34]) World Bank president Barber Conable acknowledged this as he released a study on Sub-Saharan Africa in Washington in November 1989. Many ordinary Africans, he said, "are cynical about government." Therefore, "good governance — an efficient and honest public administration — must be provided to complement policies that promote market mechanisms and entrepreneurship."[35]

Adam Smith relied on the experience of Britain when he wrote of the importance of the right to hold private property. "That security, which the laws of Great Britain give to every man that he shall enjoy the fruits of his own labor, is alone sufficient to make any country flourish."[36] Smith noted, too, that British prosperity seemed due to "the general liberty of trade" internally, to "the liberty of exporting, duty free . . . to almost any foreign country," and, perhaps more important, to "that equal and impartial administration of justice . . . which, by securing to every man the fruits of his own industry, gives the greatest and most effectual encouragement to every sort of industry."[37] Harvard economist James Bradford De Long suggests that the "key to maintaining the social capability for growth lies in a secure, predictable, and unbribable legal system; in a government that does not impose too heavy a tax burden; and in a government that does not try to direct enterprise along 'mercantilist' lines but instead lets individual entrepreneurs choose where they think their capital and energy will be most productive."[38]

Cultural Considerations

Some will argue that it is impossible to establish these political and legal conditions in Africa because the cultures of Africa will not support them. Indeed, one of the shortcomings of development assistance over the past thirty years has been the failure of international development agencies to take account of cultural differences, leading more often than not to the imposition of inappropriate policies. Western-educated African leaders were far more accepting of imported hardware and software (ideas, policies) than were the millions of people who populated the rural hinterland, and even more than those who migrated to the cities seeking the economic benefits of the modern world. Still, those who seek development for Africa do not have to look far beyond indigenous institutions to find the roots of modernization. Writes anthropologist Elliott P. Skinner: "African traditional cultures can provide the philosophical justification for looking to their own culture and existential condition for the strength to modernize."[39]

It is important to note that traditional African cultures are not adverse to the market concept. Indeed, George Ayittey, a Ghanaian-born economist now working at the Heritage Foundation, argues that other forms of economic organizations, notably socialism, are far more alien to African cultures. Before Europeans began to colonize the continent, he writes, "most of Africa had local free markets where goods were bought and sold for mutually agreed upon prices. Trans-regional trade linked distant parts of the continent."[40] The African heritage is one of self-reliance, said former Nigerian president Olusegun Obasanjo in a lecture to the Council on Foreign Relations: "Before independence, most African people had been brought up to rely almost absolutely on their environment, their maker, and their own efforts."[41]

There is little disagreement that, historically, Africans have engaged in trade and other commercial behavior. However, whether for inherent cultural reasons, because of restraints imposed by colonial powers, or because of similar restraints continued under African-born elites since independence, there has been no widespread transformation from trader to manufacturer. One participant in a Center for International Private Enterprise workshop put it this way: "Just because you're a good trader doesn't mean that you necessarily fit into the modern industrial society that most African states would like to create."[42]

It All Comes Back to Politics

Except for a few Marxist analysts who still insist on class-struggle explanations for economic phenomena, most observers agree that the transition from a commercial economy to a manufacturing one is blocked almost entirely by government policies. It is thus a political, not simply an economic problem. "The prospects for African development," writes Paul Kennedy, a social scientist at Manchester Polytechnic in England, "rest more on the exercise of political will and choice than on any other single factor."[43]

Echoing the concerns of Jane Jacobs and Deepak Lal, Professor Kennedy observes that over-emphasis on "big" projects by both African governments and the international development agencies naturally meant a neglect of small businesses that participated in whatever free market was left after the macro-managers played their hand in the economy. "Individual, micro-level, private initiatives were identified as essentially peripheral to the main thrust of development strategy."[44] It was fashionable to use aid money for heavy industry. Throughout the Third World a doctrinaire "quest for steel" took place along with the neglect of the agricultural sector and small business, leading to wasted resources and uneconomical projects.[45] Nigeria's General Obasanjo confesses on behalf of African leaders: "We opted for projects rather than programs, and the grander the projects, the more appealing they were to politicians, military men, and bureaucrats alike."[46] This relegating of the small-scale entrepreneur to the margins of development strategy stemmed from a fundamental misinterpretation of economic development history. Explains Kennedy:

The belief that nineteenth-century Western industrialization was led by powerful, rising commercial bourgeoisies who, having captured state power, were then able to remove the remaining "feudal" obstacles to full capitalist development, is almost certainly oversimplified and may even be incorrect in the case of some countries. If so, then the argument that bourgeois-led transformations are impossible in twentieth-century Africa has little historical meaning and is probably irrelevant as a reason for insisting that local capitalist groups are therefore ineligible to make some kind of contribution to capitalist development or are incapable of doing so.[47]

In post-colonial Africa, blame for lack of economic development can almost certainly be assigned to government leaders who bought wholesale the neo-Marxist explanations of their countries' economic conditions, explanations that relied on "exploitation" and made scapegoats of the West and international development agencies while fully ignoring the most likely indigenous sources of growth. Add to this the fears of dictators toward anyone or anything that might threaten their power, and the erection of barriers to economic participation by imaginative, inventive, intelligent entrepreneurs was inevitable.

Instead of creating the climate for free market growth, African leaders have been content to accept the "structural adjustment" conditions set by the World Bank and the International Monetary Fund as a strategy to solve their growing debt problem. African governments during the 1960s and 1970s borrowed billions upon billions of dollars from both private commercial banks and the international development agencies. According to the IMF, "the combined current account deficit rose from about US$4 billion in 1974 to about US$7 billion a year during 1975-77, and widened still further, reaching nearly US$10 billion annually during 1978-79. These deficits were, for the most part, financed by foreign borrowing." The total external debt increased from $15 billion at the end of 1974 to $45 billion at the end of 1979.[48] After 1980, led by the World Bank and the IMF, lending institutions insisted on certain changes in government economic policies, including the balancing of national budgets, changing tax rates, elimination of government monopolies in agriculture and manufacturing, the privatization of certain state-owned industries, and the removal of artificial constraints on prices of basic commodities.

While there is a superficial appearance of success since structural adjustment began to be the watchword, in fact economic trends in Africa have continued downward. A confidential World Bank analysis written in 1988 indicated that countries in Sub-Saharan Africa that had received structural adjustment loans had performed significantly worse than those countries that did not receive loans.[49] The World Bank's published accounts differ, however. One report focused on twenty African countries that had not been significantly affected by uncontrollable or unusual economic circumstances, such as bad weather or commodity price shocks. From 1980 to 1985, all twenty countries had similar GDP growth rates, averaging about 1.5 percent per year. In 1986-87, however, those that had pursued a structural adjustment program doubled their GDP growth rate to four percent while those without structural adjustment programs saw their GDP growth rate fall by half. [50]

David Gordon of the University of Michigan asserts that "empirically, it's obviously the case that most IMF accords are not fully implemented. Most World Bank policy-based lending programs in Africa are not fully implemented." Nonetheless, Professor Gordon says, these structural adjustment programs have "had an impact" by "putting economic reform on the map and generating some real reforms."[51] If African leaders can weather the impatience of economic and social elites (as well as peasants and workers), the full positive impact of structural adjustment will be felt. They must take into account what was pointed out by Ismail Serageldin, director of the Occidental and Central Africa Department of the World Bank: "It is an unhappy fact that the costs of adjustment have to be borne before the overall benefits become fully apparent."[52] An additional consideration was pointed out by Nigerian economist Dotun Phillips at a meeting on regional cooperation sponsored by the European Community's Center for the Development of Industry (CDI) in Lagos in April 1989. In West Africa, at least, because each state has been pursuing its adjustment programs without regard to coordination with neighboring countries, the programs have had a tendency to neutralize each other.[53]   For instance, successful import substitution in one state may hobble export promotion by its neighbor. A succinct critique of structural adjustment programs was presented by Philip Ndegwa, president of the Kenya chapter of the Society for International Development, to a meeting of development experts in Paris. Saying that he does not condemn such measures completely, he said that

(i) on their own such measures are not sufficient for the job;

(ii) the measures proposed are often expected to be implemented within entirely unrealistic time frames;

(iii) some of the measures ignore social and human consequences which then hinder further development;

(iv) some of the measures, such as those which lead to less growth and more unemployment in countries which cannot afford social security arrangements, are inappropriate;

(v) some results are unexpected and probably perverse, e.g., frequent falls in real producer food prices and destruction of small-scale low import/high labor intensity manufacturing enterprises.[54]

These are not necessarily arguments against further encouragement of structural adjustment, but they do simply point up the rocky road faced by African countries in the adjustment process, and the pitfalls that must be avoided by donor agencies if they expect structural adjustment to usher in a successful transformation of the economies of Africa and other Third World regions.

African Economic Conditions in the 1980s

One African analyst suggests that despite a few "islands of development," tropical Africa as a whole is "an ocean of adversity and decay," with an image as "the most impoverished and disordered region in the Third World."[55] Yet it has the potential of being very rich. Its natural resources are nearly unequalled. The African continent has beneath it 97 percent of the world's chrome, 85 percent of the world reserves of platinum, between 70 and 80 percent of the world's gold and diamonds, and nearly 65 percent of all manganese. Besides these mineral resources, it has substantial energy resources in the form of oil and gas and perhaps 25 percent of the potential world supply of hydroelectric power.[56]

Peter Duignan of the Hoover Institution, one of America's most respected specialists in African affairs, has noted that "in economic terms, Africa is both rich and poor; it is rich in potential resources, but it is poor if its level of economic development is compared with that of Western Europe or North America (or even with that of Asia and Latin America)."[57] The mythology that pervades many analyses of the African economic situation is that African poverty is a legacy of the colonial era. In fact, the colonial powers — for the most part — presided over unprecedented economic growth and the integration of African local economies with the world economy.

Take, for instance, the charge that the colonial powers transformed African agriculture from a system that fed the largely rural population into one that put its emphasis on cash crops for export. What actually happened was that the development of cash crops such as cocoa, rubber, cotton, and palm oil was accompanied by similar development and growth in the food crop sector. Cash crops grown for export usually signified a net increase in total agricultural output.[58] Yet since independence, outputs of both cash crops and food crops in Africa have declined; in 1960, writes Peter Duignan, "food imports accounted for less than three percent of total supplies to tropical Africa; today they account for 30 percent or more."[59] In the developed world, such a statistic might imply greater purchasing power and the reallocation of resources with better nutrition as a result. In Africa, however, it means greater debt and misallocation of resources, with lesser purchasing power and declining nutrition.

In the manufacturing and commercial sectors, those African countries that have been most successful in promoting economic growth have been those that kept intact, or nearly intact, the economic system inherited from colonial rule: Kenya, Ivory Coast, Cameroon, and Senegal are prominent examples. Those countries that destroyed the infrastructure left by colonialism also destroyed their economies. Rejection of the legal and political systems left behind by colonial rulers often meant devolution into lawlessness and disorder. Chaotic and arbitrary legal systems effectively precluded the conditions of order, stability, and predictability necessary for the maintenance of a functioning and prosperous economy.

Blanket adoption of socialist policies also led to economic and physical decay. In Mozambique, for instance, a balance of payments surplus in 1976 (one year after independence) of $41 million fell to a deficit of $244 million in 1978 and $360 million by 1980.[60] "The ideologically motivated emphasis on mechanized state farms," writes Gillian Gunn, "was disastrous. . . . It came to cost more in foreign exchange for a state farm to produce a ton of grain than it would have cost simply to import the crop."[61]

Bureaucracies grew and with them inefficiencies multiplied. Nationalization of basic industries created new opportunities for nepotism, corruption, and profit-skimming. "Most of the emergent African countries," writes Olusegun Obasanjo, "seemed to believe in development based on consumption rather than production. Large civil service bureaucracies and parastatals were built to provide unproductive jobs and to pay political debts, without taking into account the resource base that was necessary to support so unwieldy a state apparatus."[62] Africanization of the economies in most states did benefit the political elite in material terms, but not the common people. "It is not correct," writes Peter Duignan, "to trace most of the faults of African bureaucracies to the former colonial rulers." While the colonial state was similarly authoritarian and paid its bureaucrats relatively high salaries, as African states do today, it differed in that the colonial bureaucracy was "small, efficient, experienced, and rarely corrupt. The state had a limited mission during the colonial period."[63]

Duignan continues:

> In contrast, independent Africa expanded the size of its bureaucracies and enormously increased the role of the state. The size of government increased manyfold. Kenya went from a civil service of 45,000 in 1955 to 170,000 in 1984. Senegal employed 10,000 in 1960 and over 70,000 in 1984. It was not just the civil service that grew; teachers and employees of parastatals increased tenfold. In Ghana there are over 80 parastatals; Kenya has over 100; Zambia has 150; South Africa has around 300. In Africa, the people employed directly and indirectly by the state amount to possibly 50-55 percent of all working-age people.[64]

The sheer size of African bureaucracies and bureaucrats' salaries that are out of line with average income have placed a drag on African economies. Add to this the bureaucratized control of basic industries and regulations that impede the growth of the private sector both in agriculture and in manufacturing, and there is an unmistakable recipe for economic stagnation and collapse.

Moreover, African leaders made the mistake of taking as models the welfare-state economies of Western Europe and North America, where many of the most talented of them had been educated or had served in the civil service of the metropolitan power prior to independence. When they acquired power, they tried to redistribute wealth using "the textbook method of social welfarism." The failure is evident; writes Olusegun Obasanjo: "In trying to share out the unbaked cake, there being no oven available, what seems to have been distributed is poverty; and even that has been inefficiently done."[65]

According to the World Bank, "two-thirds of the rural population and a third of the urban population of Sub-Saharan Africa remain below the absolute poverty level." One common measure of poverty, infant mortality, is particularly telling: in 1985, infant mortality levels averaged 104 per thousand compared to 71 per thousand for all developing countries.[66] Life expectancy, another measure of economic health, varies widely. At the end of the 1970s, Ghanaians had a life expectancy of 45 years, Ethiopians 40, Nigerians 36, and South African blacks 59.4.[67] To give a statistical picture of Africa in 1989, U.S. AID's report to Congress for fiscal year 1990 is a good place to start. Per capita GNP for the continent as a whole is $519 (compared to $522 in 1978). Keep in mind that this aggregate figure is skewed by the inclusion of Africa's more prosperous countries in the mean: South Africa ($1,800 per capita), Mauritius ($1,200), and Congo ($1,000). All the others have per capita GNPs below $1,000; as a matter of fact, per capita GNP is Sub-Saharan Africa has a ratio of 23 to one from the richest to the poorest country.[68] At the same time, the external debt situation is dire. As a percentage of GNP, external debt for the continent amounts to 61.7 percent; as a percentage of exports, African external debt is a whopping 230.8 percent![69]

Alternatives for Economic Growth

Despite mountains of evidence to the contrary, African political leaders continue to resist change and liberalization that would lead to economic growth and development. The experience of structural adjustment programs imposed since 1980 at the urging of the World Bank and IMF has made African political elites wary of further change. After all, as Ambassador José Sorzano has pointed out, austerity measures that accompany adjustment programs "are often the functional equivalent of asking the government to commit political suicide."[70] Political leaders resist suggestions that they should open up their economies, fearing that an unbridled private sector could unleash a very real political opposition.

African finance ministers have expressed their approval of a 1989 report by the United Nations Economic Commission for Africa (ECA) titled *African Alternative Framework to Structural Adjustment Programs*. The report's chief author, Professor Adebayo Adedeji, remarked: "It has now become apparent that the orthodox structural adjustment programs that Africa has been pursuing have failed to overcome the economic crisis and in many cases have made recovery even more difficult."[71]

The ECA report attacks the adjustment programs' changes in exchange rate policies, trade liberalization, privatization, belt-tightening credit policies, interest rate increases, and allowing markets to determine prices. The report argues that trade liberalization "is not feasible in view of the protectionist practices of industrialized countries, and also because of the adverse effects of foreign competition on infant industries in Africa." It charges that privatization is impossible in an African context because it is based on "the incorrect assumption that the indigenous private sector is strong enough to take over state enterprises."[72] Privatization, the report says, "undermines growth and transformation" and "jeopardizes social welfare and the human conditions."[73]

Still, the ECA report does recognize the importance of encouraging growth in small-scale trade and industry. It calls for the "adoption of investment codes and procedures tailored to the promotion and development of small-scale industries" and for legislation that provides "a clear framework of ownership and participation of the different socio-economic groups such as rural cooperatives, artisans, traders, etc." It argues that this type of legal framework will make possible more "popular participation" in development and will strengthen the informal sector and assist that sector's "ultimate integration into the mainstream of development."[74]

Despite these bows toward free enterprise, the overarching theme of the ECA document is *dirigiste*. It is meant to serve as a counterweight to World Bank and IMF pressures to reform. It gives African finance ministers and development bureaucrats something to use as an argument against accepting conditions for development loans.

Some African development experts even disapprove of alternatives to outright economic aid, such as foreign investment in African businesses. The editors of the book *Aid and Development in Southern Africa* refer approvingly to African economists who object to "pressures by multilateral aid agencies to privatize the typical African economy" because privatization is likely to "aggravate, rather than alleviate, the causes of underdevelopment." These economists reject "the notion of foreign investment as 'aid.'"[75] The former U.S. ambassador to Nigeria, Princeton N. Lyman, has also observed this phenomenon. "It has become difficult for development practitioners and professionals," he writes, "to accept any form of economic activity not associated with (if not downright funded by) aid as truly 'developmental.'" Unfortunately, he says, this perception is not limited only to the developmentalists. The problem is that "for the U.S. public, development — rather than being an objective of distinction and value to the United States — is something that can only be achieved in these Third World countries by aid, or (to put it bluntly), charity."[76]

This makes the role of the large multilateral development banks and bilateral programs like AID's even more vital. If genuine economic reform is going to take place in Africa, the U.S. government must use all its persuasive powers, including its influence and vote in the World Bank. The main argument of this study is that the most effective persuasive tool is example: by supporting small business across the continent, U.S. AID can demonstrate that small-scale entrepreneurial activities are the engine of progress. Empirical evidence from other countries and continents, such as Taiwan or South Korea, is insufficient. African elites must be able to see success in their own backyard.

Chapter Two will examine the structure of AID and its shortcomings. It will begin the assessment of whether AID is suited to the job of creating conditions for self-sustaining economic development in Africa and other Third World regions.

Notes to Chapter One:

[1]Statement of James A. Baker, III, in *Nomination of James A. Baker III,* Hearings before the Committee on Foreign Relations, United States Senate, January 17 and 18, 1989, p. 182.

[2]"For the Record," *The Washington Post,* July 28, 1989, p. A24.

[3]Cited in José S. Sorzano, "The Revenge of the Invisible Hand," *The World & I,* Vol. 4, No. 6 (June 1989), p. 390.

[4]John Maynard Keynes, *The End of Laissez-Faire* (London: Hogarth Press, 1926), p. 12.

[5]Deepak Lal, *The Poverty of "Development Economics"* (Cambridge, Mass.: Harvard University Press, 1985), p. 108.

[6]Ibid., p. 105.

[7]Richard Sincere, "Black Market Forcing African States To Curtail Economic Restrictions," *New York City Tribune,* July 17, 1989, p. 11.

[8]"The Black Market," *African Business,* June 1989, pp. 18-22.

[9]Alfred Sayila, "Business Booms in Kenya Market," *African Business,* June 1989, p. 21.

[10]Ibid.

[11]Hernando de Soto, *The Other Path: The Invisible Revolution in the Third World* (New York: Harper and Row, 1989), p. 12.

[12]*Building Constituencies for Economic Change: Report on the International Conference on the Informal Sector* (Washington: Center for International Private Enterprise, 1987), p. 7.

[13]Ibid., p. 35.

[14]Eliana A. Cardoso, "Wrong Way," *The World & I,* Vol. 4, No. 6 (June 1989), p. 383.

[15]Edgar L. Feige, "The (Underground) Wealth of Nations," *The World & I,* Vol. 4, No. 6 (June 1989), p. 378.

[16]Interview with John Sullivan, director of public and congressional relations, Center for International Private Enterprise, July 7, 1989.

[17]Interview with Richard Bissell, assistant administrator for program and policy development, U.S. Agency for International Development, June 29, 1989.

[18]Ismail Serageldin, *Poverty, Adjustment, and Growth in Africa* (Washington: World Bank, 1989), pp. 1, 7.

[19]Nick Eberstadt, "Helping Hand Won't Solve Africa's Problems," *The Wall Street Journal*, September 17, 1987.

[20]Lal, *Poverty of "Development Economics"* , p. 103.

[21]See P. T. Bauer, *Equality, the Third World, and Economic Delusion* (Cambridge, Mass.: Harvard University Press, 1981),. pp. 177-80.

[22]H. Myint, "Economic Theory and Development Policy," *Economica*, May 1967, p. 71.

[23]Jane Jacobs, *Cities and the Wealth of Nations* (Harmondsworth, Middlesex: Penguin Books, 1986), pp. 6-7.

[24]Fanny Friedman, M.D., "Donor Policies and Third World Health," *International Health and Development*, Vol. 1, No. 2 (Summer 1989), p. 16.

[25]Ibid., p. 7

[26]"Development and Peace: An Illusory Link?," *In Brief* (U.S. Institute of Peace), July 1989, p. 1.

[27]Jacobs, *Cities and the Wealth of Nations*, pp. 221-22.

[28]Ibid., p. 221.

[29]Ibid., pp. 221-22; ellipsis in original.

[30]Lal, *Poverty of "Development Economics,"* p. 107.

[31]Elie Kedourie, "The State as Smothering Mama," *The World & I*, Vol. 4, No. 6 (June 1989), p. 402.

[32]Philip Nicolaides, "Black Marketeers Unite!," *The World & I*, Vol. 4, No. 6 (June 1989), p. 369.

[33]*See* Karl Zinsmeister, "East African Experiment: Kenyan Prosperity and Tanzanian Decline," *Journal of Economic Growth*, Vol. 2, No. 2 (1987), pp. 28-39.

[34]Vugar, Sanford J. Africa: *The People and Politics of an Emerging Continent*, New York: Simon and Shuster, 1985, p.339.

[35]Neil Henry, "World Bank Urges Steps to Reverse Africa's Economic Decline," *The Washington Post*, November 22, 1989, p. A17.

[36]Adam Smith, *An Inquiry Into the Nature and Causes of the Wealth of Nations* (Oxford: Oxford University Press, 1976), p. 540.

[37]Smith, *Wealth of Nations*, p. 610.

[38]James Bradford De Long, "The 'Protestant Ethic' Revisited: A Twentieth Century Look," *The Fletcher Forum of World Affairs*, Vol. 13, No. 2 (Summer 1989), p. 233.

[39]Elliott P. Skinner, "Development in Africa: A Cultural Perspective," *The Fletcher Forum of World Affairs*, Vol. 13, No. 2 (Summer 1989), p. 214.

[40]George B. N. Ayittey, "Restoring Africa's Free Market Tradition," *Heritage Foundation Backgrounder* No. 661, July 6, 1988, p. 1.

[41]Olusegun Obasanjo, *Africa in Perspective: Myths and Realities* (New York: Council on Foreign Relations, 1987), p. 29.

[42]Unpublished transcript, Center for International Private Enterprise, conference on "Market-Oriented Paths to Economic Growth: Lessons of the 1980s," Break-Out Session on Sub-Saharan Africa, Washington, D.C., February 15, 1989, p. 50.

[43]Paul Kennedy, *African Capitalism: The Struggle for Ascendency* (Cambridge: Cambridge University Press, 1988), p. 1.

[44]Ibid., p. 2.

[45]"Development and Peace: An Illusory Link?," p. 1.

[46]Obasanjo, *Africa in Perspective*, pp. 29-30.

[47]Kennedy, *African Capitalism*, p. 3.

[48]Justin B. Zulu and Saleh M. Nsouli, *Adjustment Programs in Africa: The Recent Experience* (Washington: International Monetary Fund, 1985), p. 1.

[49]James Bovard, "What They're Doing with Your Money Is a Crime: The World Bank," *Reason*, April 1989, p. 31.

[50]Serageldin, *Poverty, Adjustment, and Growth in Africa* , pp. 3-4.

[51]Unpublished transcript, Center for International Private Enterprise, conference on "Market-Oriented Paths to Economic Growth: Lessons of the 1980s," Break-Out Session on Sub-Saharan Africa, Washington, D.C., February 15, 1989, p. 11.

[52]Serageldin, *Poverty, Adjustment, and Growth in Africa*, p. 5.

[53]Pini Jason, "Europe's CDI urges Ecowas investment," *African Business*, June 1989, p. 17.

[54]Philip Ndegwa, "National Policies for Balanced and Sustainable Development in the Poor Countries: How to Avoid Involuntary Delinking," *Development: Journal of the Society for International Development*, No. 1 (1989)

[55]Robert H. Jackson, "Conclusion," in Peter Duignan and Robert H. Jackson, eds., *Politics and Government in African States, 1960-1985* (London: Croom Helm and Stanford, Calif.: Hoover Institution Press, 1986), p. 409.

[56]Ndegwa, "National Policies for Balanced and Sustainable Development," p. 15.

[57]Peter Duignan, "Introduction," in ibid., p. 12.

[58]Ibid., p. 14.

[59]Ibid.

[60]Gillian Gunn, "Learning from Adversity: The Mozambican Experience," in Richard J. Bloomfield, ed., *Regional Conflict and U.S. Policy: Angola and Mozambique* (Algonac, Mich.: Reference Publications, 1988), p. 153.

[61]Ibid., p. 154.

[62]Obasanjo, *Africa in Perspective*, p. 5.

[63]Duignan, "Introduction," pp. 18-19.

[64]Ibid.

[65]Obasanjo, *Africa in Perspective*, p. 35.

[66]Serageldin, *Poverty, Adjustment, and Growth in Africa* , p. 19.

[67]Richard E. Sincere, Jr., *The Politics of Sentiment: Churches and Foreign Investment in South Africa* (Washington: Ethics and Public Policy Center, 1987), p. 7.

[68]Ibid., p. 1.

[69]Agency for International Development, *Congressional Presentation Fiscal Year 1990*, Annex I, Africa, pp. 17-18.

[70]Sorzano, "Revenge of the Invisible Hand," p. 391.

[71]Cited in Michael Holman, "African plan challenges IMF line," *Financial Times* (London), July 7, 1989, p. 22.

[72]Ibid.

[73]Toby Shelley, "Answers to solutions," *West Africa*, 17-23 July 1989, p. 1161.

[74]Ibid.

[75]Denny Kalyalya, Khethiwe Mhlanga, Ann Seidman, and Joseph Semboja, eds., *Aid and Development in Southern Africa: Evaluating a Participatory Learning Process* (Trenton, N.J.: Africa World Press, 1988), p. 14.

[76]Princeton N. Lyman, "Beyond Aid: Alternative Modes of Cooperation," in Robert J. Berg and David F. Gordon, eds., *Cooperation for International Development: The United States and the Third World in the 1990s* (Boulder, Colo.: Lynne Rienner Publishers, 1989), p. 304.

Structures and Shortcomings of the

U.S. Agency for International Development

The U.S. Agency for International Development (U.S. AID) was established in 1961. In the flush of optimism that characterized the early 1960s, it was assumed that the agency would work its way out of existence within a decade or so. Those who founded AID thought that with a bit of seed money and a "trickle down" philosophy, the nations of the Third World could be launched quickly on the road to development.

In retrospect, the optimism of AID's founders seems misplaced, if not utopian. As author David Landes put it in *The New Republic*, "Economic development is not to be taken for granted. It is a hard business."[1] The challenge is made clear by the realization that AID is soon to mark its thirtieth anniversary, and the Third World is still "less developed." In fact, in some regions like Africa, economic conditions have deteriorated over the past three decades. In that thirty-year period, changing conditions and changing capabilities have caused AID's mission to be refined and redefined several times.

AID's Structure and Mission

The U.S. Agency for International Development is headquartered in Washington, D.C., with its main offices in the same building as the State Department. For this reason, it is often perceived as being part of the Department of State, although it in fact reports directly to the President as an independent agency. The headquarters houses the agency's administrator, support staff, and geographic and functional bureaus. Overseas, AID maintains over forty missions and has programs or projects in some eighty different countries.

AID administers three major programs. First is the Economic Support Fund (known as ESF), which is often considered an adjunct to national security assistance. ESF provides assistance for balance-of-payments problems, Commodity Import Program (CIP) funds, cash transfers, and various sector and project assistance. The five top recipients of ESF aid are Israel, Egypt, Pakistan, El Salvador, and the Philippines. Second, AID administers development assistance — the main focus of this study — which consists of loans and grants for projects in agriculture, nutrition, and rural development. Third, AID channels Public Law 480 (PL-480) food aid. PL-480 programs provide American agricultural products to developing countries, either through donations or through concessional sales. The Department of Agriculture works with AID in the administration of PL-480 programs.

AID is very sensitive to protecting its "turf." It has added offices and bureaus in the wake of directing legislation from Congress, which has "fostered functional redundancy or poorly defined jurisdictional boundaries." These offices were deemed necessary "for purposes of compliance, coordination or protection of turf."[2] Even when AID is supposed to cooperate with other government departments and agencies, it sometimes blocks the others' tasks and assumes them itself. Since its founding, writes development specialist Princeton Lyman, AID "has resisted independent activity in developing countries by domestic agencies such as the Agriculture and Labor departments, or the Federal Aviation Administration. At a minimum, it sought to channel such activity through its country programming and prioritization process, the more so as USAID became the source of funding such activities." Lyman complains that "this approach inevitably narrowed U.S. interaction with Third World countries. If it did not fit US-AID's priorities (which themselves shifted), it was not supportable."[3]

Four basic principles guided AID's mission during the Reagan administration, which are expected to continue during the term of President George Bush: (1) helping recipient countries with economic reforms to eliminate inappropriate policies; (2) in order to strengthen the economic capacities of developing countries, sponsoring the transfer of research and technology; (3) enhancing the growth of viable economic and social institutions that are needed to create and sustain a strong economy and free society through institution-building techniques; and (4) promoting open and competitive markets in developing countries by encouraging the growth of the private sector.

Personnel Practices

In the beginning, AID had a flexible personnel policy that was "well suited to its task," according to Boston University anthropologist Allan Hoben. Hoben explains that at the time, most AID employees were hired on a temporary basis as professionals whose "specialized skills may from time to time be required." Under this system, AID was able "to employ trained and experienced people quickly." AID employees were not required to take a civil service exam, nor did the agency assume civil service obligations. The advantages of this system included "enabling the agency to stay flexible" and providing the employees "with the incentive to maintain a professional identity."[4]

Changing requirements imposed by Congress had an effect on AID's personnel practices that did not serve the agency (or recipients of aid) well. Pressures by Congress and other executive branch units influenced AID's "organization, personnel system, work force composition, programming and contracting procedures, and incentives." Hoben notes that "its organization has become complex, inflexible, and redundant."[5] Rather than working in the field to improve development prospects, AID employees have been transfigured into bureaucrats — more concerned with process than with the end product, unwilling to take risks that might jeopardize jobs or promotions. "Regardless of their professional background," writes Hoben, "mission-based employees spend most of their time on bureaucratic and managerial tasks. Indeed, management is the only clear career ladder in the agency. Employees recruited because of other skills find it difficult to remain current in their field, to attend conferences, or to receive additional technical training."[6] The bureaucratization of

AID has caused considerable concern. Michigan State University's George H. Axinn told a congressional committee that "bureacratization of development assistance has been extremely detrimental." Axinn went so far to say that "a five-year moratorium on all foreign assistance might be healthier in the long run that further bureaucratization."[7] A study released by the Development Group for Alternative Policies (Development GAP) complained that AID employees were overpaid and this caused them to take fewer risks in program design and obstructed their creative thinking and activity. "High salaries have, as a rule, fostered more interest in job security and promotion than in the risk-taking that is an indispensable element in the provision of aid."[8]

One complaint about AID personnel is that there simply are not enough of them. A 1988 General Accounting Office report noted that AID itself believes "that inadequate numbers of direct-hire staff have affected the quality of management in many areas. The AID Inspector General has noted that the active development assistance project universe is about 2,000 — more than one project for every direct-hire employee overseas."[9] Robert Lincoln Hancock, executive vice president of Transformation International Enterprises, a non-profit development corporation based in Washington, says that AID uses "all the right language [rhetoric about free enterprise] but they don't have reliable delivery systems," that is, they don't have enough people on the ground to initiate and follow through on self-sustaining development programs.[10]

Despite these concerns, it is believed that AID's widely-dispersed personnel are an advantage to the agency and to U.S foreign policy interests. State Department officials told GAO investigators that "AID's field presence is often considered a strength of the U.S. program, particularly when compared to other bilateral donors."[11] Paul Streeten, editor of the journal *World Development*, writes that "USAID is already considerably more decentralized than, say, the World Bank or the IMF," but that further decentralization — that is, getting more people on the ground and fewer pushing papers in Washington — "can yield high returns."[12] Robert Hancock agrees: What is needed, he said in an interview, is a core of supportive service systems, that is, people on the ground to follow through. "Human contact makes the difference" in helping development projects overcome the obstacles of generally not having enough people to deliver and lack of local "ownership" of the project. ("Ownership" meaning, not just having a physical or financial stake in the project, but having an emotional stake as well — the project must make room for local initiative, creativity, and spirituality.)[13]

Use of Contractors

To supplement its direct-hire staff, AID has since its beginnings hired outside contractors to perform its tasks, particularly in the field. In fact, a 1983 GAO report said that most of AID's projects overseas were carried out through contractors. This situation has not changed.[14] Currently, AID disbursements to contractors total about $2 billion each year.[15] Allan Hoben believes that reliance on contractors for project design and follow-through creates problems. One, which is certainly not unique to AID among government agencies, is that unlike a private corporation, AID is "severely restricted in [its] ability to use generally available knowledge concerning the character, experience, knowledge, and past performance of potential contractors." The agency is forbidden "to keep systematic records of contractor performance or to use poor performance as a criterion for non-selection." About the only thing that can disqualify a contractor is "fiscal malfeasance." To prove other potentially disqualifying characteristics is difficult and time-consuming.[16] This difficultly is compounded in dealing with foreign contractors, that is, contractors hired from among local businesses in the countries where AID has projects. It is difficult to maintain any kind of quality control under the twin restrictions of government restraints and the physical distance between AID and the contractors on the ground.

What is true for some profit-making contractors is not necessarily true for charitable institutions — known as Private Voluntary Organizations (PVOs) — that work under contract to AID. As veteran diplomat and development specialist Princeton N. Lyman put it, "The United States has a concern with poverty in many parts of the world, and people-to-people relationships such as those fostered by PVOs serve many valuable ends. PVOs also provide flexibility in programming" especially "if kept distant (and they should be made more distant than they are now) from government control and cross-conditionality."[17]

However, some PVO contractors begin to depend on AID for their income and seek projects not out of a some urge to help poor people but simply to maximize their job security. The Development GAP brought this criticism to bear in a 1988 report. Some leaders of PVOs, it charged, "talk of the need to pursue AID money in order to survive, but institutional survival takes on a rather odd meaning when it includes the need to protect high salaries and to maintain what have become worldwide operations."[18] The Development GAP also argues that "AID's overfunding of a number of groups has taxed their management capabilities, changed their institutional style, and made them more bureaucratic and unresponsive to the expressed needs of the poor overseas." Citing a study sponsored by the Center of Concern, a religious think-tank based in Washington, the Development GAP complains that "PVOs often have 'lost touch with Third World realities.'"[19]

Congressional Oversight

Foreign aid has never been a favorite of most U.S. Representatives and Senators. As long ago as 1962, a Council on Foreign Relations study of the issue said that the "legislative climate . . . is far from favorable in spite of annual affirmations of the principle of foreign aid."[20] The Congressional Research Service confirmed this view in a report for the House Foreign Affairs Committee some twenty-five years later:

> From the beginning, foreign aid has never been popular in Congress. The negative reactions in Congress to the post-war continuation of Lend-Lease are an early example. Except for the first eighteen months of the Marshall Plan in Europe and for certain countries at specific times, there

has always been significant resistance in Congress to either the provision of military aid or economic aid or both.[21]

The congressional response to this fundamental "distrust" of foreign aid, as John D. Montgomery characterized it,[22] has paradoxically been to increase the intensity of congressional oversight of foreign assistance. The most common description of Congress's role in foreign aid is "micromanagement."

According to the General Accounting Office, reporting and reprogramming requirements imposed by Congress on the Agency for International Development "create a substantial administrative burden on AID and oversight burdens for Congress." A report from a development-oriented research institute noted that "in order to be responsive to Congress," AID's Washington headquarters has "imposed upon itself enormously complicated procedures which make it difficult for the field missions to be responsive to the poor."[23]

The GAO cites a report by the House Foreign Affairs Committee that said that the "level of notifications focuses congressional attention on project changes, which are inevitable, rather than on policy."[24] Long-time observer of AID Allan Hoben reports that "in 1985 alone, USAID provided 849 congressional notifications totaling 1,700 pages. The agency estimates that it devotes more than 200 person-years per year to its interaction with the Congress." As a result, complained the head of AID's Africa Bureau, "I just spend too much time fighting off the special interest brush fires . . . Clearly, effectiveness and impact suffer from all of this."[25]

David Shear, a former AID mission director in Senegal, writes that Congress's tendency toward micromanagement poses "a major constraint" on AID's "moving forward." There are, he writes, "over 106 limitations in the annual appropriations legislation, and another 100-plus in the authorizing legislation, resulting in 136 annual reports . . . The Foreign Assistance Act is now over 300 pages long, and the annual appropriations bill usually exceeds 100 pages." Shear concludes: "Such constraints constitute a major hindrance to pursuing the effective modernization of U.S. foreign assistance and its delivery systems."[26]

Under the current system, Congress oversees AID at the project level: each individual project, almost without regard to size, is subject to congressional management. Small changes in project budgets must be reported to Congress. Some analysts believe that the appropriate level for congressional review is at the country, or program, level. The GAO estimates that if AID were only required to report substantial changes at the program level, in 1987 would have had to submit about 60 percent fewer notifications to Congress — that is, 60 percent of nearly 1,200 program actions.[27]

The Development GAP, too, argues that AID deserves "far more autonomy than it presently enjoys," noting that "it is clear that Congress, since the days of the Vietnam War, has not been trusting of the executive branch's utilization of appropriated aid funds."[28] Its 1988 report, Aid for Just Development, includes a demand that "for U.S. aid to have a positive impact on development, all project aid must fall within the development assistance account and AID must be in control of both policy and administration."[29]

Such criticisms have not gone entirely unheeded. The normal congressional requirement for budgeting and notification according to "functional" accounts was waived in 1987 in response to "executive branch complaints that the functional budget categories required by the Foreign Assistance Act limited AID's operational flexibility too much." Congress, therefore, granted a single appropriation in the amount of $500 million for Sub-Saharan Africa "through a single account: Sub-Saharan Africa, development assistance." Congress authorized the funds for "any economic development assistance activities under the Foreign Assistance Act of 1961."[30]

David Shear recommends that because "micromanagement by the Congress, especially with respect to earmarking of funds, has been a major problem," the executive branch and Congress should negotiate an overall agreement that would define "the general directions of foreign assistance," create "overall policy concepts," and permit the executive branch "to undertake its work."[31] It has also been suggested that in the long run, Congress has to give AID "multiyear appropriations and more flexibility in programming these funds, while at the same time holding the agency more accountable for the developmental impact of its program."[32] In other words, for Congress to exercise its oversight obligations most effectively, it should be asking questions about whether AID programs result in sustainable development rather than demanding correct adherence to bureaucratic procedures that, it seems, stultify the agency's efforts at development rather than enhance them.

AID's Larger Mission

What is, or should be, AID's general mission in encouraging development? Many details are included in the Foreign Assistance Act and its subsequent amendments. Consequently, AID has had difficulty in keeping focus. Its personnel, funds, and management energies are dispersed too broadly. When reporting to Congress, AID's self-evaluation is based almost entirely on its meeting (on paper) the labyrinthine bureaucratic requirements that are *supposed* to assist development but are often time-consuming make-work exercises that obstruct rather than help development efforts.

Development consultant Alfred Van Huyck told staff investigators for the House Foreign Affairs Committee Task Force on Foreign Assistance that AID "overemphasizes preparation of internal documentation. It should emphasize a menu of policy and program options from which host countries can select, rather than attempting to prescribe for each country."[33]

The executive director of the U.S. Overseas Cooperative Development Committee, Ted Weihe, suggests that U.S. development assistance should focus on "'people to people' channels, supporting specific development projects through increased use of U.S. and indigenous PVOs and cooperatives," arguing that PVOs are "more effective delivery agents."[34]

The President's Commission on Privatization recommends that AID direct its policies toward encouraging privatization of nationalized industries in developing countries, supporting ESOPs (employee stock ownership plans), and work in cooperation with multilateral financial institutions and regional development banks, encouraging them to "act more decisively in private sector lending, privatization, and divestiture in less developed countries."[35]

Can AID do it? Past experience is not encouraging. Harvard economist Nick Eberstadt has criticized the agency for being "explicitly concerned ever more with relief work and social welfare, ever less with the particulars of fostering conditions conducive to 'self-sustaining economic development,'" a trend he says has been "actively and purposefully encouraged by Congress."[36] In fact, during his confirmation hearings, Secretary of State James A. Baker was confronted by Senator Gordon Humphrey (R-N.H.) on this issue. He urged Baker "to really put some emphasis on shifting our foreign assistance program in the way that we will be encouraging free enterprise and private ownership, private propert, as opposed to continuing this now decades-long cycle of assisting socialism."[37]

AID itself argues that there has been a change of attitude since the 1970s, a decade it admits produced much worth criticizing. Yet the response of the agency to questions put by the Senate Foreign Relations Committee in 1987 sound more like soothing rhetoric than a concrete commitment to policy change:

> The success of the Bureau [for Private Enterprise] in focusing the attention of the Agency on the role of private sector in development can be measured in several ways, but the ultimate test is the adoption by our overseas missions of new attitudes, the use of new programmatic mechanisms by those missions and the concomitant changes

in host government policies that lead to market driven, sustainable growth at all levels of society.[38]

With the advent of the Woods Report, it may be that AID is interested in genuine attitudinal change. Whether that is possible, given the background and make-up of current AID project officers and middle managers, is another question. The publication of the Hamilton Report by the House Foreign Affairs Committee and the submission of the Index of Economic Freedom as an amendment to the 1989 Foreign Assistance Act by Senator Connie Mack may portend a change of attitude on Capitol Hill, which would go a long way toward prodding AID to pursue successful and genuinely free-market policies in its development assistance programs.

The Problem of Evaluation

AID shares with all development agencies — whether we mean the World Bank or small church-related voluntary agencies — a problem of effective evaluation. In fact, it is extremely difficult to determine whether individual projects are successful or not. A complaint heard among Africans, for instance, is that "too often foreign 'experts' visited the projects for only a few days, talking mostly with the leaders and looking mainly at the physical aspects." These visiting experts seldom speak local languages and therefore cannot ask the poor people, whose lives are intimately affected by the aid project, whether it is helping them or whether they would like to see some alternative. Evaluation reports are "written primarily for donor organizations" and view issues "from the agencies' rather than project members' [intended beneficiaries'] perspectives." Another complaint is that qualified African researches tend to be "excluded entirely from these evaluation exercises" and consequently "neither learn from nor contribute to gathering information and designing more effective development strategies."[39]

Brian Smith, a political science professor at the Massachusetts Institute of Technology, has written that development agencies fail in self-evaluation of their projects because they do not generally devote "sufficient time or resources to conduct a thorough evaluation," they use inappropriate standards and techniques to evaluate small-scale projects, and "they have not devised methods capable of assessing intangible results like enhancement of hope and self-esteem." Moreover, these agencies avoid external evaluations because they feel "evaluation by external personnel can undermine the trust between donors and recipients." Even when external evaluators are used, "they tend to rely on evidence from the organization's staff and the projects' leaders, rather than non-leader beneficiaries or community members outside the projects."[40]

Obviously, these problems apply whether the evaluators are members of the AID Inspector General's staff or congressional investigators from the GAO or the Office of Technology Assessment. It is only natural for a Western investigator to direct his or her questions to the other Westerners involved in the project. They share the same language and, usually, the same perspective. It is complicated to speak with villagers through an interpreter. Even where Western languages are used — French, for example — the dialects spoken by Africans are often incomprehensible even to evaluators who are fluent in Parisian French but have never traveled in African countries. There is nothing necessarily sinister about this; there is no conspiracy to cover-up the failures or successes of development projects. Unfortunately, neither Congress nor the executive branch nor the general public seems interested enough to pursue an intensive, focused on-site evaluation of the range of AID projects throughout the Third World. Until that evaluation takes place, it will be difficult to assess AID's current situation and devise strategies for the future. Still, it must be admitted, bureaucrats — as so many critics say AID employees have become — are reluctant to submit to genuinely independent evaluations out of fear that their shortcomings might be uncovered, with consequences they would rather not face.

Upper-level administrators within the Agency for International Development can be surprisingly candid, however, in their assessments of how the agency is doing. After all, they would not have been appointed to their jobs if they were unwilling or incapable of pursuing the policies the administration wanted pursued. In the case of the Reagan and Bush administrations, this means pursuing private enterprise growth in developing countries and the encouragement of shrinking the public sector in favor of the private sector. Given that the obstacles to these goals present in the Third World tend to be ideological and structural ones, it should come as no surprise that AID officials appointed by Reagan and Bush are honest in their assessments.

One problem AID faces in encouraging private enterprise growth is its traditional emphasis on the rural sector. According to Richard Bissell, work in urban areas is "playing catch-up." It is important to recognize, he said, that job creation in the 1990s will be an overwhelmingly urban issue, which will require an entirely different emphasis in the structure of the agency's aid programs and strategy.[41] Another problem is a lack of focus and coordination for its microenterprise program, which AID has operated almost since the beginning of the agency. This program entails small — extremely small — grants to local businesspeople made at the mission level in local currencies, but there is no aggregate budget for this project. Assistant administrator Bissell estimates it might add up to $85 million worldwide per year — a large figure, considering most grants range from fifty cents to one dollar.

AID's efforts over the past decade have not been without their successes. The following chapters will look at AID's performance in seven African countries: Botswana, Ghana, Ivory Coast, Kenya, Senegal, South Africa, and Swaziland. Except for Ghana and Swaziland, all these countries share four characteristics that make them useful for comparisons. According to the Center for International Private Enterprise, they each have "regional weight and influence." They have established business associations with "growing membership potential among small- and medium-sized enterprises." The governments of these countries are "receptive to the private sector and [are] willing to consider market-oriented economic policy reforms." And, with the two exceptions mentioned, each has "demonstrated potential for democratic development."[42] Ghana and Swaziland have less potential for democratic development, but their economic conditions are ripe for study. Ghana is one of those countries that "hit bottom" in the early 1980s and has demonstrated remarkable — and, given the previous nature of the Jerry Rawlings regime, totally unexpected — openness to economic reform. South Africa was chosen because of its unique position as a center of political controversy and the only country where AID-administered assistance is not, under any circumstances, transferred to or through the government. Because of South Africa's regional weight, its neighbors Botswana and Swaziland were chosen for comparison and contrast. Ivory Coast has never been a major recipient of U.S. economic assistance; its performance at that minimal level will be interesting to examine. Kenya and Senegal, like Ivory Coast, are well-known as free-market-oriented states with stable governments that may prove to be models for neighboring countries.

Notes to Chapter Two:

[1] David Landes, "Rich Country, Poor Country," *The New Republic*, November 20, 1989, p. 25.

[2] Allan Hoben, "USAID: Organizational and Institutional Issues and Effectiveness," in Robert J. Berg and David F. Gordon, eds., *Cooperation for International Development: The United States and the Third World in the 1990s* (Boulder, Colo.: Lynne Rienner Publishers, 1989), pp. 257-58.

[3] Princeton N. Lyman, "Beyond Aid: Alternative Modes of Cooperation," in Berg and Gordon, eds., *Cooperation for International Development*, p. 313.

[4] Hoben, "USAID: Organizational and Institutional Issues and Effectiveness," pp. 254-55.

[5] Ibid., p. 257.

[6] Ibid., p. 259.

[7] Memo dated July 20, 1988, from Beth Ford to Lee Hamilton and Benjamin Gilman, in *Background Materials on Foreign Assistance*, Report of the Task Force on Foreign Assistance to the Committee on Foreign Affairs, U.S. House of Representatives, February 1989, p. 73.

[8] Stephen Hellinger, Douglas Hellinger, and Fred M. O'Regan, Aid for Just Development (Boulder, Colo.: Lynne Rienner Publishers, 1988), p. 30.

[9] *Foreign Aid: Problems and Issues Affecting Economic Assistance* (Washington: General Accounting Office, December 1988), p. 21.

[10] Interview with Robert Lincoln Hancock, Transformation International Enterprises, November 29, 1989

[11] *Foreign Aid: Problems and Issues Affecting Economic Assistance*, p. 24.

[12] Paul Streeten, "Accelerating Development in the Poorest Countries," in Robert J. Berg and David F. Gordon, eds., *Cooperation for International Development: The United States and the Third World in the 1990s* (Boulder, Colo.: Lynne Rienner Publishers, 1989), p. 148.

[13] Interview with Robert Lincoln Hancock, Transformation International Enterprises, November 29, 1989.

[14]Hellinger, et al, *Aid for Just Development*, p. 71.

[15]*Foreign Aid: Problems and Issues Affecting Economic Assistance*, p. 23.

[16]Hoben, "USAID: Organizational and Institutional Issues," p. 261.

[17] Lyman, "Beyond Aid: Alternative Modes of Cooperation," p. 318.

[18]Hellinger, et al., *Aid for Just Development*, p. 105.

[19]Ibid.

[20]John D. Montgomery, *The Politics of Foreign Aid* (New York: Frederick A. Praeger, 1962), p. 270.

[21]Theodor W. Galdi, "Development Assistance Policy: A Historical Overview," in *Background Materials on Foreign Assistance*, p. 256.

[22]Montgomery, *The Politics of Foreign Aid*, pp. 265-70.

[23]Hellinger, et al., *Aid for Just Development*, p. 63.

[24]U.S. General Accounting Office, *Economic Assistance: Ways to Reduce the Reprogramming Notification Burden and Improve Congressional Oversight*, September 1989, p. 7.

[25]Hoben, "USAID: Organizational and Institutional Issues," p. 273.

[26]David Shear, "U.S. Delivery Systems for International Cooperation and Development to the Year 2000," in Berg and Gordon, eds., *Cooperation for International Development*, p. 300.

[27]U.S. General Accounting Office, *Economic Assistance: Ways to Reduce the Reprogramming Notification Burden and Improve Congressional Oversight*, p. 11.

[28]Hellinger, et al., *Aid for Just Development*, p. 50.

[29]Ibid., p. 55.

[30]Galdi, "Development Assistance Policy: A Historical Overview," p. 251.

[31]Shear, "U.S. Delivery Systems for International Cooperation and Development to the Year 2000," p. 300.

3

Botswana

Botswana, a country with vast open spaces and a sparse population, is generally accepted as one of Africa's success stories, both economically and politically. Its current president, Dr. Quett Masire, was freely elected in 1980 to succeed Sir Seretse Khama, who had led the country to independence after eighty years as a British protectorate. Botswana's parliament includes members of opposition parties who take their role seriously: They question and challenge government policies.

Political stability in Botswana is helped by the relative homogeneity of the country's people. Out of a 1980 population of 936,000, the majority Batswana ethnic group numbers 910,000.[1] This has prevented the ethnic violence that has been endemic in other African countries, including neighboring South Africa and Zimbabwe. According to Hoover Institution scholars Lewis Gann and Peter Duignan, Botswana "has developed a moderate, conservative internal order that has brought stability and economic development and the rewards of foreign aid and loans."[2]

In terms of human and natural resources, the country faces several challenges. Population is increasing at a rapid rate (50.7 births per 1000 versus a death rate of 17.5 per 1000 from 1975 to 1980).[3] Only 5 percent of Botswana's 236,000 square mile territory can support agriculture; by far the largest farming pursuit is cattle raising.

Cattle raising, in fact, in many ways defines Batswana culture. One frequent visitor to the country says that the Batswana have always "loved cattle, have had a hundred ways of describing their beauty and strength." Members of parliament and civil servants raise cattle on weekends and in their spare time.[4] Nonetheless, farming and ranching do not support the entire labor force; every year, some 12 percent of Botswana's workers migrate to South Africa to seek employment.[5]

Economic Development

At independence in 1966, Botswana was a poor nation. All it had was a cattle-raising sector and a small farming sector. In fact, by most estimates, in the mid-sixties Botswana was one of the world's twenty poorest countries, but now has an economy that outperforms all the non-oil producing states of Africa.[6] Shrewd management and limited government interference in the private sector, however, created a good climate for investment and growth. From 1960 to 1969, the growth rate averaged just under 6 percent; from 1970 to 1979, the growth rate more than doubled to 13.6 percent.[7] From 1980 to 1985, the GDP growth rate was 12.1 percent, slipping to four percent in 1984-85. Over the entire period from 1965 to 1985, GDP per capita, despite a population growth rate of 3.6 percent (second highest in Africa, after Kenya), increased by 8.3 percent.[8] This was aided by an unusually high rate (for Africa) of gross domestic investment: averaging 25.9 percent for the decade ending in 1970 and 5.6 percent for the two years, 1979 and 1980.[9] The 1987-88 figures are fairly impressive, showing real GDP growth of 8.1 percent.[10]

By other standards, too, Botswana's development has been impressive. Its infant mortality rate has fallen from 98 per 1000 live births in 1966 to 65 per 1000 today, while life expectancy has increased from 35 to 60.[11]

The discovery of diamonds and other minerals substantially contributed to Botswana's economy. Yet other African countries, like Angola and Zaire, much richer in natural resources, have exhibited negative growth rates. How was Botswana able to sustain such economic success?

Ghanaian economist George Ayittey attributes the success to "judicious macroeconomic management." Although diamonds, like other mineral resources, are subject to severe ebbs and flows in the international marketplace, Botswana navigated carefully through these tides by avoiding the mistake of other African governments — it did not greatly expand the size of government (and government expenditures) during boom times. Instead, it built up its international reserves for later use during times of recession and declines in the international price of diamonds and other export commodities. During "bad times," reports Ayittey, Botswana used its accumulated reserves, reduced government spending, and adjusted its exhange rate. Political conditions, however, underlay this policy success: Botswana's "practice of open discussion . . . enabled its community to reach a consensus on appropriate policy actions."[12]

The country's bureaucracy has been efficient and relatively incorruptible. "Not all African countries would have made a deal over minerals and diamonds which meant money going clean to the Exchequer [Treasury] to be spent on such things as building roads and schools," wrote Naomi Mitchison in the *New Statesman*, a British journal of opinion. "Botswana has a fine tradition here. It is now one of the richest countries in Africa."[13] The government budget has had a surplus since 1984.[14]

The country's national development bank, the Botswana Development Corporation (BDC), has also been praised for its role in encouraging development. World Bank officials Nicholas Bruck and Paul Knotter singled out the BDC as a model for other African nations to emulate, citing its promotional activities, its efforts to attract foreign investment, its efforts to divest its shareholdings domestically, and its insistent promotion of small-scale enterprises.[15] The BDC has established a subsidiary, "Tswelelo," which is a small-scale enterprise development bank, to directly assist smaller-scale local entrepreneurs. The World Bank's *World Development Report* notes in a profile of the BDC: "BDC has been criticized for not divesting and for crowding out the private sector. However, BDC's recent initiatives have resulted in the creation of the Sechaba Investment Trust and Stockbrokers Botswana Ltd., Botswana's first investment trust company and stockbroking firm, respectively. This enables BDC to start privatizing some of its profitable companies and offers citizens an opportunity to invest in private corporations, the shares of which would not otherwise be accessible."[16]

According to *African Sunrise*, a magazine aimed at Western businessmen with an interest in Africa, Botswana's government "has recognized the necessity of a large private sector in order for the country to develop, and this state of affairs has attracted the foreign investor." The government has made it easier to obtain business residence permits, bureaucratic procedures have been loosened, and tax rates and foreign exchange procedures have been liberalized.[17]

Botswana has not been entirely immune from the problems that prey other African countries. Its bureaucracy has become increasingly powerful, assisted by foreign aid from Western donors. As a result, write Gann and Duignan, "state agencies in Botswana have become even more isolated from their respective societies than they might otherwise have been."[18]

Moreover, Botswana has a considerable employment problem. As of 1983, only 103,000 people worked in the formal sector.[19] It currently faces an unemployment rate of more than 25 percent. The rest of the labor force lacks basic skills, and because the country's two major export industries — minerals and beef — are capital-intensive, there are limited opportunities for more employment.[20] It has been estimated that each year there are 22,000 new entrants into the labor force while the formal sector creates only 7,600 jobs for them to fill.[21]

A further difficulty is Botswana's continued interdependence with South Africa's economy. President Masire told *Leadership*, a South African journal: "Botswana buys most of its goods in South Africa. If we were to buy these goods from countries further than South Africa they would be more expensive. Similarly, the proximity of South African ports and their efficiency means that it is cheaper for Botswana to use them."[22] Botswana is tied to South Africa in a customs union established in 1969, and it is not always happy with the arrangement, claiming that it (and Lesotho and Swaziland, the other members of the customs union) subsidizes South African industry by buying 90 percent of their import quotas from South Africa, which charges high prices due to its own stringent import quotas. There is also a complaint that South Africa does not make its revenue payments (tariffs and taxes) within a reasonable amount of time, often delaying payment by two to three years.[23] The imposition of international economic sanctions on South Africa has also contributed to an economic slump in the countries bordering South Africa.

The Role of U.S. Development Assistance

From 1965 to 1982, total U.S. development assistance to Botswana was about $130 million.[24] One successful project supported by the U.S. Agency for International Development in the recent past is the Technology Center, which encourages small entrepreneurs whose businesses use simple technologies that are easily obtained. The intention is to use local resources that depend on ingenuity and skill rather than to rely on imports dispersed in the domestic market.[25]

AID's plans for the future are closely coordinated with the government of Botswana. It aims to address the employment problems through education, assistance to the private sector, and programs to improve productivity and self-sufficiency among smallholding farmers. AID claims that as a direct result of its activities, "well-trained Batswana have begun to replace expatriates [mostly British and South African] in key positions in the government and the private sector."[26]

In conjunction with the Botswana government, AID sponsored a study aimed at stimulating the growth of the private sector. "Many of the recommendations of the study on policies and procedures to stimulate greater use of market forces," AID reports, "have been formally espoused by the government."[27] AID has also been supporting efforts of the International Executive Service Corps, a private voluntary organization, which is working with private firms to improve private sector productivity. In addition, to assist the growing private sector home construction industry, AID has supported the construction of 7,000 low-cost houses.[28]

AID's request for assistance to Botswana for fiscal year 1990 is $7 million, the bulk of which will go towards education projects.[29]

Assessment for the Future

Botswana has certain characteristics that, given the proper level of development assistance to the nascent private sector, could make it a model of economic success. The Botswana government is already inclined toward the market, despite its heavy investment in the diamond industry (the state owns about 50 percent, with the South African giant De Beers owning the rest). The Botswana Enterprises Development Program is designed to stimulate private business through training, tax holidays, capital grants to small enterprises to create new jobs, and capital grants for agribusiness.[30]

This openness to the private sector, which includes a desire to integrate the formal and informal business sectors, makes Botswana particularly ripe for assistance from the United States, whether through AID's Bureau of Private Enterprise or through the Center for International Private Enterprise, which channels funds from the National Endowment for Democracy.

Some experts warn that political frictions — brewing disputes between native Batswana and expatriate workers and entrepreneurs, between the civil service and the private sector, between the few minorities and the majority Batswana, and between rural and urban interests — may jeopardize the stability that has been built since independence. The government, luckily, is aware of the potential disruptions and is putting its energies into strengthening the private sector, which in turn will be a major part of the foundation for sustaining democracy.

Notes to Chapter Three:

[1]U.S. Department of State, Bureau of Public Affairs, *Background Notes: Botswana*, May 1983, pp. 1-2.

[2]L. H. Gann and Peter Duignan, "Namibia, Botswana, Lesotho, and Swaziland," in Peter Duignan and Robert H. Jackson, eds., *Politics and Government in African States 1960-1985* (London: Croom Helm and Stanford, Calif.: Hoover Institution Press, 1987), p. 366.

[3] Ibid., p. 365.

[4]Naomi Mitchison, "Diamonds and cows," *New Statesman* (London), 26 February 1988, pp. 24-25.

[5]Gann and Duignan, "Namibia, Botswana, Lesotho, and Swaziland," p. 365.

[6]Frances Paine, "Botswana boom," *African Sunrise*, Vol. 3, No. 2 (1989), p. 32.

[7]Ibid., pp. 367-68.

[8]John D. Sullivan, unpublished memorandum for the Center for International Private Enterprise, "Trip Report: Kenya, South Africa, Botswana, Nigeria, June 20 to July 2, 1988," July 30, 1988, p. 30.

[9]Gann and Duignan, "Namibia, Botswana, Lesotho, and Swaziland," p. 368.

[10]"Windfalls from the desert," *African Sunrise*, Vol. 3, No. 2 (1989), p. 36.

[11]Michael Holmes, "Diamonds and Dust," *Leadership South Africa*, Vol. 6, No. 4 (1987), p. 50.

[12]George B. N. Ayittey, "The Political Economy of Reform in Africa," *Journal of Economic Growth*, Vol. 3, No. 3 (Spring 1989), p. 5.

[13]Mitchison, "Diamonds and cows," p. 25.

[14]"Windfalls from the desert," p. 36.

[15]"World Bank praises Botswana bank," *African Business*, June 1989, p. 24.

[16]Ibid., p. 29.

[17]Paine, "Botswana boom," p. 34.

[18]Gann and Duignan, "Namibia, Botswana, Lesotho, and Swaziland," p. 369.

[19]U.S. Department of State, *Background Notes: Botswana*, p. 1.

[20]U.S. Agency for International Development, *Congressional Presentation, Fiscal Year 1990, Annex I, Africa*, p. 45.

[21]Sullivan, "Trip Report," p. 31.

[22]"Man in Conflict," *Leadership South Africa*, Vol. 6, No. 4 (1987), p. 44.

[23]Gann and Duignan, "Namibia, Botswana, Lesotho, and Swaziland," p. 374.

[24]U.S. Department of State, *Background Notes: Botswana*, p. 4.

[25]Paul Kennedy, *African Capitalism : The Struggle for Ascendancy* (Cambridge: Cambridge University Press, 1988), p. 190.

[26]U.S. Agency for International Development, *Congressional Presentation*, p. 46.

[27]Ibid.

[28]Ibid., pp. 46-47.

[29]Ibid., p. 47.

[30]Sullivan, "Trip Report," p. 32.

4

Ivory Coast

Ivory Coast (Cote d'Ivoire) is widely touted as one of Africa's economic success stories. Its history since independence has been one of political stability that engendered growth. However, more recent developments point to a decidedly more pessimistic view of the future. The Ivoirian government, buoyant from the success of the 1960s and early 1970s, has begun to intrude on the economy and as a result, stagnation is occurring.

Under President Felix Houphouet-Boigny, who is now well into his eighties if not past 90, Ivory Coast has enjoyed unusual stability and continuity of competent leadership. Before independence, Houphouet-Boigny had been a minister in the government of the French Fourth Republic. He negotiated Ivoirian independence from a position of strength and influence, and has maintained good relations with France ever since; in fact, there are more French citizens living and working in Ivory Coast today than there were in the colonial era. This has been part of a deliberate government policy. In a speech before the Organization of African Unity's heads of state, President Houphouet-Boigny said:

> It is true, dear colleagues, that there are 40,000 Frenchmen in my country and that is more than there were before Independence. But in ten years I hope the position will be different. I hope that then there will be 100,000 Frenchmen here. And I would like at that time to meet again and compare the economic strength of your countries with mine. But I fear, dear colleagues, that few of you will be in a position to attend.[1]

In an area slightly larger than New Mexico, Ivory Coast supports a population of about nine million. The annual population growth rate is 3.5 percent. Its main exports are coffee, cocoa, timber, rubber, palm oil, and pineapples.

A recent curiosity has brought Ivory Coast to the attention of the world. As an act of personal piety, President Houphouet-Boigny is building what is believed to be the world's largest basilica (although the official, tactful word is that it is slightly smaller than St. Peter's Basilica in Rome). Built at a cost of $250 million — reportedly from the president's personal funds — the Basilica of Our Lady of Peace towers over Yamoussoukro, Houphouet-Boigny's home village and the country's newly-designated capital city. The large cost at a time of economic retrenchment is probably the reason Pope John Paul II declined an invitation to dedicate the basilica himself.[2]

Houphouet-Boigny's advancing age has made the question of succession a very real one for Ivoirian politics. The favorite to succeed the country's first and only president is the president of the National Assembly, Henri Konan Bedie. It appears that the succession, whenever it occurs, will be smooth. What happens after that is harder to predict.

Economic Development

For most of the post-colonial era, Ivory Coast has been a model of development. Boasting one of Africa's most comprehensive transport and communication networks, it is the most highly industrialized black African country after Zimbabwe and Nigeria, and is certainly one of the continent's most diversified economies.[3] Its net economic growth rate stood at about 5 percent until the mid-1980s. Most of this growth, however, was due to the momentum set in the 1960s, when free-market policies predominated and foreign and domestic investment was high. Looking at a narrower window — 1973 to 1985 — the Ivoirian real GNP growth was negative, averaging -1.1 percent per year. After rising steadily for fifteen years, since 1980 per capita income has fallen at a similar rate, so that by 1986 it was only $740.[4]

How did this occur, given that as late as 1978 the World Bank published a book called *Ivory Coast: The Challenge of Success?* Simply put, in the mid-1970s, Ivory Coast began to adopt some of the statist policies that had condemned its neighbors to perpetual poverty. Until 1973, Ivory Coast relied almost exclusively on market forces to regulate the economy. In that year, however, it adopted a national five-year plan that signified "the government's desire to become more actively involved in the allocation of resources through investment."[5]

A state agency, known by its French initials as CSSPPA, became the only authorized buyer of coffee and cocoa, the most important export crops. It was able to maintain an average annual budget surplus of $349 million, which allowed the government to increase its investments in other sectors of the economy. In fact, public sector investment in the economy outpaced private investment. This had severe consequences for the way investment decisions were made.

According to economist Pascal Wick, civil servants who did not bear the conseqences or responsibilities of their decisions began to direct the economy. Bad decisions became more common, such as one to build six sugar refineries in the northern part of the economy that have become a major drain on the government's agriculture budget.

As the negative consequences of increased government intervention in the economy began to be felt, the government response was not to decrease such intervention, but to increase it even more. A system of tariffs and import/export controls had the effect of discouraging exports. Overregulation "diminished the incentive [in local firms] to move towards more efficient production."[6] The overall effect of the combined state interventions was to undermine Ivoirian growth potential. Public debt increased dramatically, growing from about 24 percent of GDP in 1975 to nearly 50 percent in 1980. In 1981, therefore, the Ivoirian government went to the IMF and World Bank for assistance.[7]

The loans were conditioned on basic institutional reforms, including reducing the public sector deficit and reaching near-equilibrium in the balance of payments. By 1983, the country had to reschedule its debt because none of the objectives of the earlier agreement had been met. Unlike private industry faced with a similar situation, the government was safe: "There was no 'bankruptcy,' no thoroughgoing restructuring, and no change of management as there would have been if decisionmakers were held accountable."[8]

The story of Ivory Coast's self-imposed recession is clearly one of the economic consequences of political decisions. In the late colonial period and early post-independence period the country had respected property rights, held down taxes, and created a climate of stability and security for investment. Then, in 1973, the government shifted course. Increased regulation, intervention in foreign trade, and government agricultural monopolies made investment insecure. Economic growth failed to continue.

The Role of U.S. Development Aid

Apparently, the U.S. Agency for International Development still believes that Ivory Coast is a model for development. Its expenditures on foreign assistance there amount to barely $500,000, most of it channeled into family planning programs. It has no program to assist small- or medium-sized businesses.[9]

AID maintains its regional headquarters in Abidjan, the port city that used to be the Ivoirian capital, so there is no excuse for U.S. development officials to be unaware of the country's decline.

Assessment for the Future

Despite prodding by the World Bank and the IMF, Ivory Coast shows little inclination for significant economic reform. This is a shame, because its earlier performance demonstrates that the Ivoirian people have the capacity for capitalist expansion and the generation of economic growth.

The World Bank has established a program to give money to assist micro-enterprises in the informal sector as well as "a smallholder credit scheme in the rubber sector, improved agricultural extension for small farmers, increased water supply connections to poverty areas, [and] a rural roads upgrading and rehabilitation program."[10]

Perhaps in the regime that will follow the passing of Houphouet-Boigny there will be a return to the free-market policies that characterized the early years of his government. Unfortunately, it appears that "the Old Man" has left his pragmatic self behind and has become set in his statist, interventionist ways, to the detriment of the Ivoirian economy and to the disadvantage of the country's people.

Notes to Chapter Four:

[1] Quoted in Paul Johnson, *Modern Times: The World from the Twenties to the Eighties* (New York: Harper and Row, 1983), p. 527.

[2] Howard Schissel, "Bursting with its own power — a glimpse of Africa," *African Sunrise*, Vol. 3, No. 1 (1989), pp. 14-15.

[3] Victor T. Le Vine, "Cameroon, Togo, and the States of Formerly French West Africa," in Peter Duignan and Robert H. Jackson, *Politics and Government in African States 1960-1985* (London: Croom Helm and Stanford, Calif.: Hoover Institution Press, 1987), p. 108.

[4] U.S. Agency for International Development, *Congressional Presentation, Fiscal Year 1990, Annex I, Africa*, pp. 120-21.

[5] Pascal Wick, "The Role of Government in the Economic Recession of Cote d'Ivoire," *Journal of Economic Growth*, Vol. 3, No. 3 (Spring 1989), p. 40.

[6] Ibid., p. 44.

[7] Ibid., p. 45.

[8] Ibid., p. 46.

[9] U.S. Agency for International Development, *Congressional Presentation*, pp. 122-23.

[10] Ismail Serageldin, *Poverty, Adjustment, and Growth in Africa* (Washington: World Bank, 1989), p. 51.

5

Ghana

Ghana was the first of the Sub-Saharan African states to become independent of its colonial rulers. As the Gold Coast, Ghana was one of the jewels in the British imperial crown. In thirty-two years since independence, all that former glory has been lost. First, under the regime of the charismatic Kwame Nkrumah, who preached, "Seek ye first the political kingdom," the economic infrastructure that had been established during the colonial era was allowed to crumble; statist policies destroyed indigenous African businesses and the generations-old market sector. After Nkrumah was deposed, successive military dictatorships and interludes of weak civilian rule did little to improve the situation.

Ghana's population of 14 million is expected to double by the year 2000. Its main export is cocoa, originally brought to the country by enterprising Ghanaian farmers in defiance of colonial regulations. Cocoa amounts to 54.4 percent of total exports. It also exports minerals such as gold, aluminum, diamonds, and manganese.

The country is currently under scrutiny because of the Economic Recovery Program launched by the regime of Flight Lieutenant Jerry Rawlings in 1983. Since the recovery plan began, GDP growth rates have improved to 6 percent per year, after more than ten years of negative growth. (Between 1985 and 1988, Ghana's per capita growth rate averaged 1.8 percent.[1]) In part because of Ghana's historical stature as the first independent African country and in part simply because of the vast size of its recovery program, the World Bank has noted that "other African countries are watching Ghana's experience with great interest. It is in effect a bellwether of how serious donors are about supporting major sub-Saharan reform efforts."[2]

Economic Development

At the time of independence, Ghana had a higher standard of living than Portugal, which was itself then the colonial master of several African countries. It had the best roads, ports, schools, and hospitals in colonial Africa, and foreign exchange reserves of nearly $500 million.[3] Kwame Nkrumah, the Western-educated politician who had led the country to independence, was in an enviable position.

However, Nkrumah despised free enterprise. "We would be hampering our advance to socialism if we were to encourage the growth of Ghanaian private capitalism in our midst," he said, and proceeded to nationalize most of the economy and decree legislation that made business almost impossible to pursue.[4] Over time, the bureaucratization of the economy destroyed the economy. As one analyst explained: "The parastatals were, and are, extravagant, incompetent, and nepotistic. Despite the arguable relevance of doctrinaire public sector dirigisme, they have become millstones around Ghana's economic neck. They constitute a burden from which the country has been utterly unable to release itself."[5]

Some of the examples of Nkrumah's excesses are, in retrospect, comic. For instance, with the help of Soviet-bloc money, he built an ultra-modern mango cannery. Besides the fact that few mango trees grew in Ghana, the plant's capacity exceeded the entire worldwide demand for mangos. A gold mine in Bibiana employed several hundred workers well into the 1970s, although the last bit of gold ore had been dug out in 1968. One report suggested that by keeping the mine open, "the cost was five times what it would have taken to pay every worker the minimum wage for staying at home."[6]

Ghana's cocoa production fell from 340,000 metric tons in 1973 to 277,000 tons in 1977. Inflation and unemployment set off civil strife. Real wages fell 80 percent between 1974 and 1985.[7]

Under Nkrumah and successive regimes, Ghana's formal sector shrank. People escaped into the informal economy, called *Kalabule*. Instead of growing cocoa for export through the government's marketing board, peasants began growing foodstuffs or, if they continued to put their energies into cocoa, they smuggled it across the border. The irony was that as the state tried to gain firmer control over the economy, the economy simply slipped through its fingers. Manchester Polytechnic's Paul Kennedy explains: "Paradoxically, . . . in extreme cases, one of the major consequences of statism — in addition to economic stagnation and even decline — is that the state loses much of its control over the formal economy anyway, and therefore its ability to obtain revenue and direct resources whether for productive or essentially parasitical purposes."[8]

Jerry Rawlings led two military coups, first in 1979 and again in late 1981, to combat the excesses of bad government. By 1983, when he turned to the World Bank and International Monetary Fund for assistance, "there was just no viable alternative strategy available"[9] — at least no socialist strategy. The economy had reached rock bottom and "had nowhere to go but up."[10] So far, that assessment seems correct. The *Financial Times* reported in mid-1989 that real GDP grew 5 percent per year since 1983 and real per capita incomes have increased by 15 percent. Cocoa exports are on the rise again, predicted to be 291,000 tons in 1989, almost double the 1984 export crop of 149,000 tons.[11] In addition, inflation shrank from 120 percent in 1983 to about 30 percent by 1987.[12]

Structural adjustment has been substantial but not complete. The government now sets prices for only five commodities; it used to set them for 6,000 commodities. The bloated bureaucracy has been reduced and divested. Tens of thousands of civil servants were sacked, adding to a growing unemployment problem. The labor force is growing at 3.75 percent a year against a population growth rate of less than 3 percent. Over the next three years it is expected 60,000 government workers will be seeking new employment; one estimate is that there will be a need to create over 200,000 new jobs by 1992.[13]

In the all-important cocoa industry, however, the government retains a firm grip. It still will only guarantee 50 percent of the world price of cocoa to Ghana's farmers, who therefore have fewer reasons to work hard and produce more cocoa. Kwame Owusu, chief executive of the Ghana Cocoa Board, argues that "cocoa gives Ghana about 60 percent of its foreign exchange. Should we let the private man decide when he wants to sell his cocoa? How does the Ghana government get the money to let the nation live?"[14]

Ghanaian-born economist George Ayittey is not too optimistic about the country's reform package. He told a Center for International Private Enterprise conference of his August 1988 visit to his native land. "I don't want to sound too negative," he said, "but I was looking very hard to see some signs of progress in Ghana; there wasn't any."[15] The problem Professor Ayittey sees is political. After years of military regimes and several coups, he has little confidence that another coup will not overthrow the Rawlings regime because some military leaders view the current reforms with disfavor. "The scenario is not hard to imagine," he told *Insight* magazine. "Some leftist idiot overthrows Rawlings and says Ghana has been sold off to the imperialists. Everything the government is doing is thrown overboard, and that's it for Ghana."[16]

A study report prepared for the House Foreign Affairs Committee reached similar conclusions: "In Ghana, most high officials, trade union leaders, and academic experts appreciated the potential of structural adjustment for promoting greater economic efficiency and growth. But they agreed that the average urban-dweller did not perceive that he or she was currently benefiting from the program. One leading official acknowledged that, were it put to a popular vote in the cities, the economic reform program would lose. . . . Many observers felt that an eventual economic downturn, accompanied by rising democratic expectations, could threaten the adjustment program and ultimately the existing government."[17]

These views make potential foreign investors nervous — and domestic investors, too. Businessmen, reports the *Financial Times*, think that private investment will not take off until "the government signals its good intentions, possibly by inviting the multinationals to buy back at least some of the equity in their enterprises that they [had been] forced to sell in the 1970s."[18] The chairman of the Ghana Employers' Association, former Nkrumah cabinet minister James Phillips, notes that "private companies are contracting. Many are cutting their payrolls with voluntary retrenchment schemes," in part because of a lack of credit availability.[19] Overregulation also contributes to the absence of new investment. The head of the Ghana Investment Center admits that administrative delays, such as project approvals that take as long as six or eight months, have caused a decline in project approvals from 94 percent in 1986 to 60 percent in 1988. Moreover, foreign investors are discouraged by a requirement that, for a project to be 100 percent foreign-owned, it must be a new venture and must demonstrate that it will be a net foreign exchange partner. Otherwise, the foreign investor must find both a Ghanaian partner in the venture and a substantial source of Ghanaian finance for the project.[20]

The Role of U.S. Development Assistance

One British journalist has called Ghana "a development worker's paradise." Multilateral and bilateral donors are jockeying for position, trying to stake their claim in Ghana's incipient success story.[21] Development agencies want to use Ghana as a "showcase of cures for what ails the Third World." Seung Choi, the World Bank's Ghana chief, says that "this experiment is sending a very important message. It shows that the countries of Africa are coming to grips with reality."[22] (The fact that Ghana is under analysis in this book is itself due to the development community's pride in the country; until Richard Bissell of the U.S. Agency for International Development recommended its inclusion among the countries examined here, Ghana was going to be left out.[23])

In its budget request for fiscal year 1990, U.S. AID explains that "the goal of AID assistance for the 1988-90 period is to contribute to an increase in Ghanaian per capita income growth."[24] AID programs will focus on the agricultural sector, because that sector has the most potential for private sector employment generation. They will also assist Ghanaian workers displaced by the privatization of state-owned enterprises, using local currencies to support such activities as rural credit and community-led initiatives and to improve social services and physical infrastructure.[25]

AID will provide training to public sector employees under the rubric of the Human Resources Development Assistance project, to improve their abilities to carry out the responsibilities of the Economic Recovery Program. At the same time, it will train private sector workers in methods to better take advantage of the opportunities offered by the Economic Recovery Program.[26]

Using P.L.480 commodities, AID will generate local currency from their sale and channel those funds into employment generation programs in the private sector.

AID's 1988 expenditures in Ghana amounted to just over $22 million. Expected 1989 assistance is nearly $26 million; the fiscal year 1990 request is $26.7 million.[27]

The House Foreign Affairs Committee study mission to Ghana in late 1988 questioned whether AID's efforts — and those of other donor agencies — "will be sufficient to significantly alleviate rural poverty." As an example, the study mission report pointed to AID's Agricultural Productivity Promotion Program, which emphasizes privatization and gives additional support for extension services and feeder roads, but "ignores the entire issue of women in agriculture." An AID official told the investigators: "This project was just a 'tail on' to what the World Bank was doing."[28]

Assessment for the Future

Reckless rhetoric from the Rawlings regime may discourage most private investors from the West away from Ghana, but the creative disarray since 1983 is making many opportunities possible that would have been unthinkable a decade ago. For instance, Ghanaian lobstermen are now sending their produce to Europe. Other non-traditional exports that are just getting off the ground are processed goods like furniture, aluminum products, and canned fish, in addition to small-scale products like handicrafts, textiles, and wood carvings.[29]

There are, however, obstacles to further development of these non-traditional export industries. Ghana has no viable packaging industry, for instance, and suffers from poor transportation, an absence of export marketing expertise, and competition from neighboring countries who are trying to develop the same new markets for non-traditional exports.[30]

The greatest obstacle to further development remains international uncertainty about the future of the Rawlings regime. To satisfy a strong Marxist element within his government, Rawlings continues to excoriate the United States and the West in the United Nations. He personally and literally embraces world figures like Fidel Castro and Moammar Gaddafi. As one Western diplomat in Accra told the *Washington Post:* "Ghana goes out of its way to spit on the United States and kick it in the shins."[31] One result of Rawlings radicalism was a cut in U.S. foreign assistance (in 1986) from an original figure of $23 million to $14 million. Said another Western diplomat: "The Ghanaians are shooting themselves in the foot every morning, as far as U.S. support is concerned."[32]

Rawlings may be viewed as a pragmatist, but he is still a dedicated revolutionary. At a ceremony marking the tenth anniversary of his original coup d'état, Rawlings said: "In our tradition an act of abomination can only be washed away by blood. Not out of vindictiveness but because only blood which is life can wash away sin."[33] Considering that the Rawlings regime began with a purge of the entrepreneurial class, beating and shooting those who violated government-imposed price controls, and taking a bulldozer to Accra's famous Makola Market, words such as this can hardly instill confidence in businesspeople. Despite Ghana's pride of place in the annals of the development industry, it will be a long time before we can say with any certainty that economic liberalism has taken firm and permanent root.

Notes to Chapter Five:

[1] *Structural Adjustment in Africa: Insights from the Experiences of Ghana and Senegal*, Report of a Study Mission to Great Britain, Ghana, Senegal, Cote d'Ivoire, and France, Nov. 29-Dec. 20, 1988, to the Committee on Foreign Affiars, U.S. House of Representatives, March 1989, p. 6.

[2] Cited in Holman Jenkins, "Ghana on a Road to Freer Economy," *Insight*, September 12, 1988, p. 10.

[3] Holman Jenkins, "How Africa's 'Black Star' Burned Out on Statism," *Insight*, September 12, 1988, p. 11.

[4] Ibid., p. 14.

[5] A. H. M. Kirk-Greene, "West Africa: Nigeria and Ghana," in Peter Duignan and Robert H. Jackson, eds., *Politics and Government in African States 1960-1985* (London: Croom Helm and Stanford, Calif.: Hoover Institution Press, 1987), p. 41.

[6] Jenkins, "How Africa's 'Black Star' Burned Out," p. 13.

[7] Kirk-Greene, "West Africa," pp. 42-43.

[8] Paul Kennedy, *African Capitalism: The Struggle for Ascendancy* (Cambridge: Cambridge University Press, 1988), p. 77.

[9] Tony Hawkins, "Star pupil comes of age," *Financial Times* (London), Section III, p. 1.

[10] Ibid.

[11] Ibid.

[12] U.S. Agency for International Development, *Congressional Presentation, Fiscal Year 1990, Annex I, Africa*, p. 153.

[13] Tony Hawkins, "Tackling the costs of growth," *Financial Times* (London), July 11, 1989, Section III, p. 4. A study mission of the House Foreign Affairs Committee estimates that 80,000 government workers have been fired or will soon lose their jobs as part of the structural adjustment program; see *Structural Adjustment in Africa: Insights from the Experiences of Ghana and Senegal*, p. 2.

[14]Holman Jenkins, "Crusader's Bitter Medicine Enlivens Nation's Revival," *Insight*, September 12, 1988, p. 16.

[15]Unpublished transcript, Center for International Private Enterprise conference on "Market-Oriented Paths to Economic Growth: Lessons of the 1980s," break-out session on sub-Saharan Africa, Washington, D.C., February 15, 1989, pp. 15-16.

[16]Jenkins, "Ghana on a Road to Freer Economy," p. 10.

[17]*tructural Adjustment in Africa: Insights from the Experiences of Ghana and Senegal*, pp. 15-16.

[18]Hawkins, "Star pupil comes of age," Section III, p. 1.

[19]Jenkins, "Crusader's Bitter Medicine," p. 17.

[20]Tony Hawkins, "First shots in investment war," *Financial Times* (London), July 11, 1989, Section III, p. 3.

[21]William Keeling, "Development worker's paradise," *Financial Times* (London), July 11, 1989, Section III, p. 6.

[22]Jenkins, "Ghana on a Road to Freer Economy," p. 8.

[23]Interview with Richard Bissell, assistant administrator for programs and planning, U.S. Agency for International Development, June 29, 1989.

[24]U.S. Agency for International Development, *Congressional Presentation*, p. 153.

[25]Ibid., p. 154.

[26]Ibid., p. 155.

[27]Ibid., p. 152.

[28]*Structural Adjustment in Africa: Insights from the Experiences of Ghana and Senegal*, p. 9.

[29]John Tanner, "Let them eat lobster," *African Sunrise*, Vol. 3, No. 1 (1989), pp. 41-42.

[30]Tony Hawkins, "Drive to develop non-traditional exports," *Financial Times* (London), July 11, 1989, Section III, p. 2.

[31]Blaine Harden, "Ghana Mixes Capitalism, Radical Foreign Policy," *The Washington Post*, August 24, 1986.

[32]Ibid.

[33]William Keeling, "A pragmatic leadership," *Financial Times* (London), July 11, 1989, Section III, p. 2.

6

Kenya

If any country in Africa is a success story, Kenya is arguably it. Kenya's post-independence governments made a conscious choice to retain the infrastructure and philosophy that had been established by the British colonial regime. Under Jomo Kenyatta, the country's first president, Kenya rejected nationalization, centralization, and the confiscation of private property. In fact, private property ownership was encouraged and individual enterprise was viewed as the best means to eliminate poverty.[1]

Kenya has Africa's fastest growing population and one of its smallest ratios of arable land per citizen. The official estimate of Kenya's population is 20 to 22 million, growing at a rate of 4 percent per year; some analysts expect, however, that a forthcoming census will uncover a total population of 35 to 40 million.[2]

Kenya has a potential workforce of about eight million people, of whom between 10 and 15 percent are employed in the formal sector. This large percentage of workers in the informal sector causes the Kenyan government to take the informal economy very seriously, indeed. A report from the Ministry of Planning and National Development suggests that by the year 2000, 75 percent of all new urban jobs will be in the informal sector.[3] This includes absorbing 300,000 school-leavers each year.[4] The government is putting considerable efforts and energies into improving the efficiency and productivity of the informal sector, including an investment of nearly $13 million in infrastructure facilities, not only in the cities but in small towns and rural areas. The Ministry of Industry has distributed a booklet aimed at educating the public about the assistance available for informal sector development.[5]

There are very pragmatic reasons for this, as the chief economist for the Ministry of Planning and National Development explained to a conference audience in Washington in late 1987:

We have to create employment opportunities for ten million people ten years from now. The formal sector requires some $20,000 to create one job. That is a lot of money, given the resources at the disposal of the Kenyan government. However, the corresponding job created in the informal sector costs less than $5,000. This suggests that if we have to make an impact in terms of employment creation, more attention should be put on the informal sector.[6]

This eminently practical approach towards the informal sector should come as no surprise to the student of Kenyan history, for it is just another example of the adaptability and flexibility shown by the Kenyan government toward the economy since independence was declared in 1963.

Economic Development

From the beginning, the Kenyan government was "wedded to the goal of productivity pursued through market mechanisms."[7] The transition from a colonial settler society to one controlled by Africans was smooth. President Kenyatta oversaw the Africanization of the agricultural sector with no sacrifice of productivity. Some 70,000 African families took possession of two million acres of fertile land; the existence of such smallholdings proved to be a powerful stimulus to rural free enterprise development.[8]

Kenyan agricultural output has grown by an average of 4 percent per year since independence. The most important reason is that "Kenyan farmers earn the prevailing world market price for their export crops." Because Kenyan farmers are paid on this basis, they are able to make intelligent' decisions based on the information they receive through the global information network known as the market.[9] Moreover, throughout the post-independence period, the tax burden on Kenyan farmers has been moderately low and therefore has not discouraged production as in other African states.[10]

Kenya's economic success has not been without cost. Political friction involving the country's Asian minorities led to outright persecution of Asian shopkeepers, manufacturers, and entrepreneurs. The state used licensing laws to restrict Asian trade; in the process, politicians and civil servants became wealthy by acting as silent partners — "fronts" — for Asian businessmen in return for their patronage and protection against official harassment.[11] Karl Zinsmeister argues that the pressure against Asians "not only damages economic activity directly, it also makes Kenyans of Asian origin nervous about reinvesting in their own country. As a result, there is a damaging flight of both capital and human skills from the country."[12]

Kenya's per capita GNP has been growing steadily but in small increments since 1963, about 2 percent per year. In 1986, per capita income was $300.[13] In 1988, real GDP rose by 5.2 percent, compared to 4.8 percent in 1987.[14] Despite this small per capita GNP, Kenya is generally recognized as "an astonishing exception" on the African continent.[15] According to Africa specialists Robert H. Jackson and Carl G. Rosberg, among the former British colonies of East Africa:

> Kenya alone has achieved considerable post-independence success in both political and economic development by avoiding the destructive ethnopolitical warfare of Uganda and the rationalist utopianism of Tanzania. Kenya managed to establish effective political institutions that contributed to political stability while nevertheless permitting a moderate degree of authentic democracy within a one-party framework."[16]

During 1988, according to University of Nairobi economist G. K. Ikiara, Kenya's industrial sector grew by 6 percent, "the highest since 1979," and the agricultural growth rate was 4.4 percent, up from 1987's 3.8 percent. Also, the gross fixed investment rate in 1988 was an "impressive" 9 percent."[17]

The Role of U.S. Development Aid

Kenya must be a favorite of U.S. development officials. Programs there are used over and over again as examples in the 1987 U.S. AID publication, *Economic Growth and the Third World: A Report on the AID Private Enterprise Initiative.* For instance:

"Small farmers in Kenya, because of AID's Rural Private Enterprise Project, are growing, harvesting, and selling oil seed for the first time; higher income is being created for about 6,000 families."[18]

Or: "AID has helped Kenya increase productivity on its small farms by supporting policy changes such as reducing government involvement inthe economy and providing access to agricultural supplies and markets. For example, the Kenyan government's policy of limiting fertilizer imports was reversed, thereby substantially increasing maize output and reducing food imports."[19]

And again: The Bureau of Private Enterprise (PRE) "provided $2.75 million to the Kenya Commercial Bank and the Kenya Commercial Finance Company to secure business expansion loans to small- and medium-size enterprises. One beneficiary was Kenby Cables, a small firm that makes about 20 types of copper cables for residential and industrial wiring. . . . Kenby Cables now employs 25 more people and produces cable for customers who formerly relied on imports."[20]

Other examples include a $2 million PRE loan to Leather Industries of Kenya, which will enable it to process 1,000 hides a day, or 25 percent of the country's raw leather production[21] and AID's Rural Private Enterprise Project's intention to make small loans to labor-intensive rural enterprises, with a goal of creating 7,000 jobs.[22]

With the assistance of AID, the Kenyan government has launched a program aiming to foster small-scale rural businesses in metal fabrication, food processing, and providing farm supplies. Also with AID's help, the Kenyan Commercial Bank has developed a plan to help micro-businesses that cannot obtain normal financial assistance from banks as well as those whose proprietors lack basic accounting and management skills.[23]

AID's development strategy for Kenya over the next ten years will focus on "expanding the role of the private sector in the economy." Through the Economic Support Fund, P.L. 480, and the Development Fund for Africa, AID will "support sectoral reforms for the private sector . . . [and] will support agro-industrial enterprises, investment support services, rural enterprise marketing, and other investments which have a major employment-generation effect."[24]

In fiscal year 1988, AID spent a total of $52.2 million in Kenya; the budget for 1989 is $46.7 million, while the budget request for fiscal year 1990 is $51.3 million. Four million dollars is budgeted for the Kenya Market Development Program, and $7 million is intended to support private sector policy reforms, with another $7 million going to general Private Enterprise Development.[25]

Assessment for the Future

Unlike so many Third World countries that repress and discourage the informal sector, Kenya shines bright in its encouragement of informal private sector growth. In what other country would the president visit a major informal sector market? Daniel arap Moi did just that in 1986 when he visited Nairobi's Gikomba market, a gathering place for many *jua kali* (Kiswahili for "hot sun," indicating that the work is done in the open air) artisans.[26]

The Kenyan government intends to help informal sector manufacturers find export markets for their products. It has built worksheds for *jua kali* businesses and has assisted in the establishment of cooperatives and credit societies.[27] Thus the assessment of John Sullivan of the Center for International Private Enterprise should come as no surprise: "Informal manufacturers are now coming to be seen by the Kenyan government as an asset rather than a liability due to the need to generate employment."[28]

Nonetheless, most of Kenya's informal businesses that have succeeded have done so without direct government aid. The Ministry of Planning and National Development reported in 1988 that:

the private sector, and in particular the small enterprise sector, has continued to grow without the benefit of direct government assistance. A survey of 1,500 small enterprises indicated that none of them had benefited from any direct government program. Government should therefore change the focus of its strategy away from direct intervention (in the economy) to one of facilitating private sector initiative.[29]

Kenya is probably ready for an indigenous organization like Hernando de Soto's Institute for Liberty and Democracy to help spread the gospel of informal sector economics. Nairobi should become a magnet-school for African entrepreneurs. To a certain extent, this has been recognized by U.S. AID, which in fact early in 1989 sponsored a conference in Nairobi at which de Soto delivered a major address. However, if there is to be found anywhere in Africa a spokesman for the informal sector, Kenya will probably be the place.

Notes to Chapter Six:

[1] Karl Zinsmeister, "East African Experiment: Kenyan Prosperity and Tanzanian Decline," *Journal of Economic Growth*, Vol. 2, No. 2 (1987), pp. 28-29.

[2] John D. Sullivan, unpublished memorandum, "Trip Report: Kenya, South Africa, Botswana, Nigeria, June 20 to July 2, 1988," Center for International Private Enterprise, July 30, 1988, p. 6.

[3] Center for International Private Enterprise, *Informal Sector Newsletter*, July 1989, p. 1.

[4] Brian Onyango, "*Jua Kali* seeks PTA markets," *African Business*, August 1989, p. 24.

[5] Remarks of Dr. I. Onyango, *Building Constituencies for Economic Change: Report on the International Conference on the Informal Sector* (Washington: Center for International Private Enterprise, 1987), p. 35.

[6] Ibid.

[7] Robert H. Jackson and Carl G. Rosberg, "The States of East Africa: Tanzania, Uganda, and Kenya," in Peter Duignan and Robert H. Jackson, eds., *Politics and Government in African States 1960-1985* (London: Croom Helm and Stanford, Calif.: Hoover Institution Press, 1987), p. 235.

[8] Ibid., p. 234.

[9] Zinsmeister, "East African Experiment," p. 30.

[10] Jackson and Rosberg, "The States of East Africa," p. 235.

[11] Ibid., p. 236.

[12] Zinsmeister, "East African Experiment," p. 37.

[13] U.S. Agency for International Development, *Congressional Presentation, Fiscal Year 1990, Annex I, Africa*, p. 180.

[14]G. K. Ikiara, "Growth continues despite obstacles," *African Business*, August 1989, p. 21.

[15]Zinsmeister, "East African Experiment," p. 337.

[16]Jackson and Rosberg, "The States of East Africa," p. 244.

[17]Ikiara, "Growth continues despite obstacles," p. 21.

[18]U.S. Agency for International Development, *Economic Growth and the Third World: A Report on the AID Private Enterprise Initiative*, April 1987, p. 3.

[19]Ibid., p. 15.

[20]Ibid., pp. 17-18.

[21]Ibid., p. 22.

[22]Ibid., p. 23.

[23]Paul Kennedy, *African Capitalism: The Struggle for Ascendancy* (Cambridge: Cambridge University Press, 1988), p. 190.

[24]U.S. Agency for International Development, *Congressional Presentation*, pp. 183-84.

[25]Ibid., pp. 182, 185.

[26]Shadrack Amakoye, "Blessing to backstreet entrepreneurs," *African Sunrise*, Vol. 3, No. 1 (1989), p. 40.

[27]Ibid., p. 41.

[28]Sullivan, unpublished memorandum, p. 7.

[29]*Informal Sector Newsletter*, July 1989, p. 7.

7

Senegal

Charles Bray, a former U.S. ambassador to Senegal, once called the country "the Costa Rica of Africa." Ambassador Bray based his assessment on the fact that "the law rules; the dignity and integrity of the individual are respected; there is no torture; there are no political prisoners."[1]

A country of six million people with a territory about the size of South Dakota, Senegal is indeed one of Africa's political success stories. Fifteen parties compete for seats in the National Assembly. National politics, however, is dominated by the Socialist Party founded by Senegal's first president, Leopold Senghor, who in 1981 retired voluntarily, the first African civilian leader to leave office voluntarily and peacefully. His successor, Abdou Diouf, was elected from a field of five candidates in 1983 with more than 80 percent of the vote.

Senegal was in the headlines in 1989 because of troubles with neighboring Mauritania. The problem centered on resentment on both sides of the border towards nationals from each country living and working in the other. In Mauritania, several Senegalese were killed. Thousands of Mauritanian shopkeepers were airlifted out of Dakar, the capital of Senegal, leaving a commercial vacuum and providing a field day for looters. Altogether, almost half a million Mauritanians were repatriated, which sent shockwaves through Senegal's economy.[2] One consequence of the strife was the cancellation of a meeting of the New York-based Africa Travel Association that had been scheduled for May 1989 in Dakar.[3]

Such civil unrest, however, has been rare in Senegal. As a result, the country has had steady but low-level economic growth, the low level probably a reflection of the socialist policies initiated during Senghor's twenty-year administration.

Economic Development

Senegal's growth rate has averaged 2.3 percent since independence in 1960, one of the lowest in Francophone Africa and, according to the U.S. Agency for International Development, "the lowest rate of any sub-Saharan state not affected by war or political strife."[4] Its per capita GNP ($420) is a little over half that of nearby Ivory Coast.[5] It is one of a handful of African countries where per capita income was about the same in 1985 as it was in 1960.[6] One factor may have been the large growth in government; in just thirteen years, from independence in 1960 to 1973, the number of government employees ballooned from 10,000 to 61,000.[7]

Poorly-written and badly-implemented legislation has also played a part. For instance, a 1972 investment code intended to encourage Senegalese entrepreneurs ended up aiding instead the French and Lebanese expatriate investors the government wanted to displace. According to Manchester Polytechnic's Paul Kennedy, the law set the amount of minimum investment necessary to qualify for loans "too high and [the benefits were] therefore inaccessible to the majority of Senegalese entrepreneurs."[8] (Economically speaking, this result was neither positive nor negative; an investor is an investor. Politically, however, such a result is problematic for the government that drafts the law in the face of fear and envy of foreigners among the domestic population.) In addition, the government imposed heavy taxes and obtrusive regulations.[9]

In the 1970s and early 1980s, Senegal often acted to suppress the private sector. For instance, SOTRAC, the public bus system in Dakar, has operated with a budget deficit of about 25 percent while handling about 20 percent of passenger trips in the region. Another 40 percent of the passengers are carried by an informal, private sector system called *Cars Rapides*. Government regulations, however, prevented the expansion of *Cars Rapides* during the 1970s in order to protect SOTRAC's official monopoly. Despite its deficit, the government proposed in 1981 to expand SOTRAC at a cost of $61 million and to ban *Cars Rapides*, which, according to development expert Elliot Berg, "carries twice as many passengers as do the SOTRAC buses, and has done so without government subsidy and in the face of government restrictions on fleet expansion."[10]

The disproportionately large size of the agricultural sector in Senegal's economy has also been a drag on development, compounded by inefficient government policies. Michigan State University professor Carl K. Eicher wrote in 1986: "Senegal's failure to get its agriculture moving during the twenty years of Senghor's regime and the five years under President Diouf has imposed a severe hardship on the welfare of the population and has been a severe brake on the entire economy."[11]

In 1984, Senegal introduced free market economic reforms both in agriculture and in industry and commerce. For most of its history, the state had played a large and direct role in the marketing of agricultural products — particularly the country's biggest export, groundnuts — in most cases actually monopolizing trade. A "New Agricultural Policy" was introduced in 1984; the ultimate aim of the policy is 100 percent food self-sufficiency, with a short-range goal of 75 percent sufficiency in food grains by the year 2000. The policy has expanded the role of the private sector in food production, encouraging the growth of farmers' cooperatives in both inputs and outputs, and it has reduced the role played by parastatals and state-run development authorities.[12]

So far this policy has been only partially successful. Groundnut production has increased markedly, from 576,000 tons in 1985-86 to 946,450 tons in 1987-88; after a slight drop in 1986-87, cotton output increased over the same period from 30,000 tons to 36,000 tons. However, food grain production has actually decreased. Millet production fell from 950,000 tons in 1985-86 to 800,000 tons in 1987-88; rice production came down from 147,000 tons to 136,000 tons; and the maize harvest was reduced from 146,500 tons to 113,600 tons, dipping even lower (to 108,000 tons) in 1986-87.[13] Unable to feed itself, Senegal was forced to import 274,000 tons of rice in 1988 and 110,000 tons of wheat the same year.[14]

At the same time the New Agricultural Policy was introduced, Senegal launched its New Industrial Policy (NIP). The NIP was meant to promote the private sector by reducing government involvement in the economy. According to a report in African Business, "Measures designed to encourage the private sector — such as cutting production costs, diversifying industry, increasing research and development, and improving investments and exports — have lagged behind the implementation of more damaging measures, such as exposing local firms to outside competition by abolishing import barriers."[15] Industries seeking to improve production sometimes must depend on smugglers to provide them with basic supplies, such as tin cans in food processing factories.

Despite some setbacks, the reform seems to be working. Since 1985, economic growth has averaged more than 4.2 percent annually and inflation fell from 12.5 percent to 1.1 percent in 1987 and consumer prices may even start falling in the near future. The state sector is shrinking, with the number of government employees falling from 72,000 to 68,000.[16]

However, the government faces growing dissatisfaction and political opposition as a result of implementing structural adjustment reforms. A study mission of the House Foreign Affairs Committee reported in early 1989 that "the urban impact of adjustment presented the governing party in 1988 with its most serious challenge since independence." By complaining about "ultraliberalism" and unemployment, reduced subsidies for consumers, and higher prices along with reduced government services, "the opposition picked up considerable electoral support, especially in urban areas." The study mission asserted that "Senegal was traversing a political crisis that threatened both the existing adjustment program and a unique brand of African democracy."[17]

The Role of U.S. Development Aid

These improving conditions make the possibilities of successful assistance for the private sector from U.S. AID very good. Since the beginning of Senegal's economic reform program, AID has been pursuing "an aggressive policy dialogue aimed at reducing the role of the state and promoting the free play of market forces."[18] The goals of this dialogue have included "improvement of fiscal performance, with allocation of resources to productive sectors; implementation of a coherent strategy for increased food security; liberalization of cereals marketing; promotion of the private sector as a substitute for defunct government agencies . . . ; reduction of the role of agricultural development agencies; and restoration of bank liquidity and use of better banking practices."[19]

AID has initiated vigorous assistance to the private sector. A pilot credit program under the Community and Enterprise Development Project has loaned more than $1 million to over 300 small enterprises, primarily in rural areas. Ninety-eight percent of the loans have been paid back when due.[20]

AID's budget for Senegal is fluctuating. In 1988, $30,813,000 was spent; the estimated expenditure for 1989 is $47,000,000; but the amount requested for fiscal year 1990 is only $37,000,000. Fifteen million dollars will be directed to structural reforms in industry and agriculture. The informal sector will benefit from small amounts allocated for self-help measures and local currency programming.[21]

The House Foreign Affairs Committee study mission to Senegal criticized AID's efforts there, saying that "many informed observers are skeptical that small farmers will find this system [a revolving credit fund for private suppliers of fertilizers and other inputs] very accessible in the absence of major changes in adjustment policies dealing with producer credit or crop pricing."[22]

Assessment for the Future

As one observer has put it, "Senegal has turned out to be an undoubted political success story; whether it can also turn the economic corner is open to debate."[23] A lot will depend on the success of the economic reforms launched in 1984 and encouraged by U.S. AID, as well as by the World Bank and IMF. Senegal's government has shown remarkable pragmatism despite the ruling party's philosophical commitment to socialism. This pragmatism was probably inherited from Leopold Senghor, who is unique among African leaders in his literary career (as a poet, Senghor won a coveted membership in the Academie Francaise). Senghor told an American journalist that "the first task of socialism is not to create social justice. It is to establish working democracies."[24] It would serve Africa well if this idea of Senghor's swept the continent as rapidly and as comprehensively as his conception of "Negritude" did in the 1940s and '50s.

Unlike some other African countries, Senegal seems genuinely committed to the structural adjustment program it adopted in the mid-1980s under pressure from the international lending agencies. There has been some backsliding, of course. The lifting of price controls has been slipshod and ineffective. As in other African countries, competing elements of the structural adjustment program have led to contradictory policies. For example, from the start the Senegalese government has tried to pay farmers the world market price for their produce; at the same time, it has had to keep down food prices in the cities in order to prevent inflation and unrest among the urban citizens, whose wages could not keep up with the prices paid to the farmers.[25]

One glimmer of hope may lie in the tourist industry, which currently constitutes 13 percent of export earnings and is the most profitable segment of Senegal's economy.[26] Senegal has been offering travelers the opportunity to live among African villagers in a traditional setting in a program called "integrated tourism," which was described by a French journalist as "exemplary, for it has improved life in the villages without introducing many of the noxious effects generally associated with Western tourism in the Third World." During 1988, more than 20,000 tourists visited the integrated tourism camps.[27] In 1988 a plan was announced by the Organization of African Unity to erect a $500 million memorial to the slave trade near Dakar, which would include not just a monument but a permanent research institution, the Institute for the Study of Slavery. Gorée Island, two miles off Dakar in the Atlantic Ocean, was a processing center for more than 20 million African slaves between the sixteenth and nineteenth centuries, of which two million ended up in North America.[28] Clearly, this kind of historical center could attract many American tourists and researchers, especially black Americans interested in understanding their roots. Though it might seem frivolous to some, U.S. foreign assistance directed at the development of the Senegalese tourist industry would be money well spent. The building of a tourist infrastructure — hotels, airports, taxicabs, laundry services, restaurants — is simultaneously the building of an inviting climate for businessmen and investors.

There are obstacles to overcome. Dakar's airport, for instance, has notoriously bad service. Having a boarding pass does not guarantee a seat on the airplane. "If you are one of the unlucky passengers with boarding passes (it's 'free seating') but left roaming the aisles when all the seats have been occupied," writes a journalist who visited Dakar in early 1989, "then you have to get back off and take some other flight — which is, of course, much more easily said than done."[29] If U.S. AID can import some technical and managerial experts to assist the reorganization of Yoff Airport, Senegal could enter the 1990s at the top of the list of tourist destinations for African travellers.

Notes to Chapter Six:

[1] Cited in Gerard Alexander, "African Success Stories," *Policy Review*, Spring 1986, p. 52.

[2] Mary Harper, "Departed Mauritanians leave trade vacuum," *African Business*, July 1989, pp. 44-45.

[3] Linda Van Buren, "US travel group cancels Senegal trip," *African Business*, June 1989, p. 36.

[4] U.S. Agency for International Development, *Congressional Presentation Fiscal Year 1990, Annex I, Africa*, p. 313.

[5] Ibid., p. 310.

[6] Carl K. Eicher, "Strategic Issues in Combating Hunger and Poverty in Africa," in Robert J. Berg and Jennifer Seymour Whitaker, eds., *Strategies for African Development* (Berkeley: University of California Press, 1986), p.260.

[7] Crawford Young, "Africa's Colonial Legacy," in Berg and Whitaker, eds., *Strategies for African Development* , p. 43.

[8] Paul Kennedy, *African Capitalism: The Struggle for Ascendancy* (Cambridge: Cambridge University Press, 1988), p. 69.

[9] Alexander, "African Success Stories," p. 52.

[10] Elliot Berg, "Private Sector Potential in Africa," *Journal of Economic Growth*, Vol. 1, No. 3 (1986), p. 21.

[11] Eicher, "Strategic Issues in Combating Hunger and Poverty," p.

[12] Ibid., p.259.

[13] Harper, "Departed Mauritanians leave trade vacuum," p. 44.

[14] Ibid., p. 45.

[15] Ibid.

[16]U.S. Agency for International Development, *Congressional Presentation*, p. 314.

[17]*Structural Adjustment in Africa: Insights from the Experiences of Ghana and Senegal*, Report of a Study Mission to Great Britain, Ghana, Senegal, Cote d'Ivoire, and France, Nov. 29-Dec. 20, 1988, to the Committee on Foreign Affiars, U.S. House of Representatives, March 1989, p. 16.

[18]Ibid., p. 313.

[19]Ibid.

[20]Ibid., p. 315.

[21]Ibid., pp. 312, 315.

[22]*Structural Adjustment in Africa: Insights from the Experiences of Ghana and Senegal*, p. 13.

[23]Victor T. Le Vine, "Cameroon, Togo, and the States of Formerly French West Africa," in Peter Duignan and Robert H. Jackson, *Politics and Government in African States 1960-1985* (London: Croom Helm and Stanford, Calif.: Hoover Institution Press, 1987), p. 108.

[24]Cited in Alexander, "African Success Stories," p. 52.

[25]Eicher, "Strategies for Combating Hunger and Poverty," p. 259.

[26]Harper, "Departed Mauritanians leave trade vacuum," p. 45.

[27]Howard Schissel, "Integrated tourism," *African Sunrise*, Vol. 3, No. 2 (1989), p. 25.

[28]Paul Lewis, "Memorial to the Slave Trade Planned for Senegal," *The New York Times*, October 5, 1988, p. A9.

[29]Van Buren, "US travel group cancels Senegal trip," p. 36.

8

South Africa

The recent political and economic history of South Africa is so well-known it probably needs no rehearsing here. South Africa remains the only African country south of the Sahara that is politically dominated by a white minority. Through the system called apartheid, or separate development, black South Africans have been denied full participation in the democratic structures open to other South Africans.

Currently, South Africa is undergoing dynamic change. The eleven-year-old government of State President P. W. Botha — who came to power as prime minister in 1978 and later, under a new constitution that was drafted under his direction, became president in what political scientists would call a "strong executive" form of government — was forced to leave office in August 1989. In Botha's place is F. W. de Klerk, a much younger man who promises a quickening pace of reform.

Unlike most other African countries, South Africa is a target of opprobrium in the West. Except for Libya, no other African state is the subject of U.S. economic sanctions. The sanctions debate has, in fact, dominated discussions of U.S.-South African relations over the past ten years. It can even be said that sanctions and apartheid have dominated discussions of U.S.-*African* relations, almost to the exclusion of the rest of the continent!

Economic Development

Economically, South Africa is the powerhouse of Africa. It has the world's largest known deposits of chromium, manganese, platinum, vanadium, and gold, as well as major reserves of other valuable minerals such as asbestos, coal, copper, diamonds, iron, nickel, phosphates silver, uranium, and zinc. South Africa produces more than 75 percent of Africa's steel and more than 50 percent of the continent's electrical power. Its neighboring countries — particularly Botswana, Lesotho, and Swaziland, the so-called "BLS" states — are inextricably tied to South Africa in transport, communications, and energy supplies.

South Africa has enjoyed sustained economic growth over the past forty years that began to slow in the early 1980s. From 1951 to 1961, the country's Gross Domestic Product (GDP) grew annually by an average of 4.3 percent. From 1961 to 1971, this figure grew to 4.9 percent, then fell to 3.3 percent between 1971 and 1981. Since 1981, in the words of one South African economist, "the economy has been treading water, with an annual real growth averaging less than one half of a percentage point."[1]

South Africa's economy is one of the most socialized outside the Communist bloc. This may come as a surprise to anti-apartheid activists outside South Africa, who base their case for punitive economic sanctions on the "fact" that capitalism and apartheid are allies. Undercutting the economy, these activists say, would pull the rug out from the apartheid system and destroy white rule. In fact, apartheid is a form of ethnic socialism. As Walter Kansteiner of the Institute on Religion and Democracy has put it:

> The National Party was a 'volk' or people-oriented party whose primary objective was to look after the welfare of the Afrikaner. Highly nationalistic with very real tendencies toward a centrally-planned economy, the 'Nats' built a government bureaucracy that provided thousands of jobs to their volk. In creating this pref-

erential world, the National Party embraced the policy of 'apartheid' or separate development. Blacks were restricted in where they could live, what jobs they could hold, and who they could marry."[2]

As Afrikaners moved from the farms to the cities in the 1930s and 1940s in response to the worldwide Depression and the Second World War, the need for jobs stimulated the growth of the National Party, which had had limited electoral success against the United Party of Field Marshal Jan Smuts — a hero of both the Second Anglo-Boer War (1899-1903) and the First World War — who had been able to lead a coalition of English- and Afrikaans-speaking South Africans. The demographic and social changes of the 1940s, however, led to a breakdown of Smuts' influence, and his party was narrowly defeated at the polls in 1948 by Daniel F. Malan's Nationalists. Once in power, the Nationalists through patronage and initial adherence to the tenets of apartheid were able to maintain a majority in the South African parliament. By the 1970s, the United Party was phased out, replaced by the Progressive Federal Party and other small groups of liberals.

High on the agenda of the Nationalists was the creation of job security for the party's supporters. This took two forms. One was the establishment of state-owned corporations in such sectors as steel, communications, arms, and energy. The other was legislation that reserved certain occupations for whites. These job reservation laws, now fully repealed, were a cornerstone of apartheid. They deliberately prevented the economic advance of blacks, coloureds (people of mixed racial background), and Asians. Other laws soon followed: influx control regulations to limit the free movement of labor; laws preventing blacks from owning commercial and homestead property; laws segregating the workplace; laws mandating, again purposefully, substantially inferior schools for blacks, in order to keep them in a servile state.

The Nationalists were fully aware of the economic consequences of these acts. Hendrik Verwoerd was fond of saying that, for him and his people, "given a choice between a rich, integrated society and an impoverished, segregated society, [we] will choose an impoverished, segregated society." For various pseudosociological and religious reasons, which have since been rejected by most South African elites (including the incumbent National Party leadership), social segregation was seen as more important than economic growth and prosperity. It was not long before the world took note of the anomalous and cruel situation that had arisen in South Africa. By the mid-1960s, a worldwide campaign for economic sanctions was underway. The sanctions campaign clearly had an impact on South African economic thinking. It stimulated a *laager* philosophy (a *laager* is the Afrikaner equivalent of the Old West's "circling the wagons") that advocated economic autarky. Firm and substantial efforts were made to reduce South Africa's dependence on imports, particularly of strategic substances like petroleum and other energy products. Home-grown substitutes were encouraged. Nonetheless, throughout the 1960s and 70s, right through to the imposition of severe sanctions by the United States in 1986, international trade grew and remained a significant sector of the economy.[3] However, as the economy frayed around the edges because of the threat of sanctions and other factors (the drop in gold prices and the rise in oil prices worldwide, among others), it became clear to South African policymakers that something must be done to encourage economic growth. The result was an end to the most universally condemned forms of economic and social apartheid.

The late 1970s saw the legalization of black trade unions, perhaps the most potent force for change in South Africa today. By 1988, job reservation laws, influx control (the infamous "pass laws"), restrictions on home ownership, and similar laws had been consigned to the legislative junk pile. The most significant aspects of apartheid that remained were mostly social or political, such as the Group Areas Act, which segregates living areas according to race, and the continued denial of the right to vote in national elections for black citizens. The National Party government expressed a commitment to improve black education, not for altruistic reasons, but for pragmatic ones: South Africa needs literate, trained, and skilled workers and managers, and there simply are not enough white people to fill the need. Though most of the most overtly racist economic laws and regulations have been repealed in recent years, South Africa remains overregulated. Although among business people and many free-enterprise oriented anti-apartheid activists there is a strong and broad consensus in favor of deregulation, "certain forces within the white community . . . lack enthusiasm" for it, according to financial writer Robin Friedland. These forces include "ideological extremists who still adhere to the Verwoerdian tenet that urban blacks are mere 'temporary sojourners'" in the urban areas; "civil servants who may feel that any move away from a *dirigiste* system threatens their own function and tenure of office;" and white trade union members who "object to [solutions to] certain problems of small business which require relaxation of aspects of labor law for their mitigation."[4]

Nonetheless, in some areas at least, the informal sector has been growing apace and fighting regulation along the way. For example, blacks are no longer forbidden to open a business, either in the segregated townships or in the central business districts of the main cities (Johannesburg, Durban, Cape Town). However, red tape and lack of access to start-up capital continue to pose significant barriers.[5]

For years South African black workers had no choice about how they travelled to their jobs: either walk or take the bus, owned by the state monopoly SATS (South African Transportation Service, which also owns the state airline, SAA). Bus fares were high relative to incomes; many people chose to walk for several hours each way. Then some enterprising young blacks started a taxi service. A few cars and vans grew into dozens; dozens grew into hundreds. Today, the taxis operated by the Southern African Black Taxi Association (SABTA) are the second-largest users of oil and gasoline in South Africa, after the government itself. The sheer size of SABTA's business forced the government first to ignore, then to repeal, the regulation that forbade competition with the state-owned transport system. Taxi drivers are now among the entrepreneurial class and drive more than passengers — by their example and their accumulation of capital, they are driving the local economies. Spinoffs from the taxi business already include service stations, car washes, and steam-cleaning operations; plans for the future include participation in the tourist industry by bringing foreigners to the townships on tours led by the black residents rather than white outsiders.[6]

Another set of regulations deals with hawkers and street venders. If a person wants to set up a roadside stand selling, say, vegetables or umbrellas, he must first publish a notice of his intent to do so in a local newspaper. Any business located within a short distance of the intended hawker's stand — about 100 yards — can then object to the proposal, asking the local council not to issue a business permit. Specious reasons are often given, such as "disrupting vehicular and pedestrian traffic," but the real reason is almost always that the already-established business does not want to face competition. Moreover, local regulations also require that roadside hawkers move their stands every two hours and then not return to the same site within twenty-four hours. Common sense shows that this is no way to start a business. An effective response to these Kafkaesque regulations has begun. Lawrence Mavundla, a young former labor organizer, established ACHIB — the African Council of Hawkers and Informal Business — which represents the hawkers before local councils, argues their case for reduced regulation, and helps raise capital to start small businesses. The basic start-up loan is often no more than about $135, but to an unemployed black South African it can be a life's savings.

Mavundla's group has met limited success, mostly with the more liberal councils in the Johannesburg and Cape Town areas, but the problem is national in scope and requires national legislation to solve it. Members of Mavundla's organization have a lot to show for their efforts. Although most began with little more than a table and a few second-hand goods, some have already been able to open real shops that compete with white- and Indian-owned businesses. (A great deal of resentment remains among township blacks toward Indian merchants, who were granted a near-monopoly in township commerce by the government during the 1960s and 1970s.)

Hawkers generate, according to one estimate, more than a billion rand — $500 million — into the South African economy. Still another estimate suggests that the informal sector in South Africa amounts to about 40 percent of the economy, employing between 3.5 and 4 million people, and earning between $3.6 and $4.7 billion each year.[7] They are emerging as the most recent members of a growing black middle class, which had mostly been made up of athletes and performers, teachers, a handful of lawyers and physicians, and managers promoted by large multinational corporations that abided by the Sullivan Principles of racial non-discrimination. For the first time, substantial wealth is actually being created rather than simply redistributed within the black community. This is a major step forward; in political terms, it gives blacks a visible stake in stability and peaceful change.[8] As Mavundla argues, "The hungry cannot be fed words, they must be given the freedom and means to pull themselves up, and then they can discuss politics."[9]

Former State Department official Alan Keyes has argued forcefully in congressional testimony that the sanctions track the U.S. government has been on since 1986 is mistaken and should be replaced by a program of investment in black empowerment. He told a 1987 Senate Foreign Relations Committee hearing: "The challenge of democracy in South Africa is precisely the challenge of popular empowerment. This challenge should not be a secondary goal or an afterthought, but the primary focus and direction of our resources."[10] In later testimony before the House Africa Subcommittee, Keyes asserted that "our aim should be to harness the energy and resources of the private sector to the task of positive empowerment for black South Africans. Black entrepreneurs and managers, in positions of real authority, represent positive power. A massive effort should be taken to develop such individuals."[11]

The Role of U.S. Development Aid

South Africa is unique in that U.S. economic assistance there is not part of a government-to-government transfer. In fact, because of the strength of the South African economy, for many years there was no U.S. development assistance directed there. There was no AID mission, no Peace Corps contingent, and — given the United Nations arms embargo in force since the early 1960s — certainly no security assistance.

With the passage of the Comprehensive Anti-Apartheid Act of 1986 (CAAA, or "C-Triple-A"), however, which mandated certain economic sanctions against South Africa, development assistance for the first time became a reality. In this case, though, U.S. AID efforts must be directed to "victims of apartheid" — presumably almost exclusively black South Africans. In practice, critics of the sanctions legislation say, U.S. development assistance in South Africa is in fact helping defray the costs of U.S. policy by aiding the "victims of sanctions." Charles W. Freeman, Jr., deputy assistant secretary of state for African affairs in the Reagan administration, defined AID's role in testimony before the House Africa Subcommittee in 1988. AID programs, he said in response to a question from Representative Dan Burton (R-Ind.), "are directed to assisting victims of apartheid in a variety of ways. They pay legal fees for detainees, and they pay for the sustenance of the detainees' families. They pay to train South African black lawyers in civil rights law. They pay for scholarships for black South Africans in many, many disciplines. They pay for community development projects. And finally, they pay for black business development projects."[12]

The U.S. ambassador in South Africa, even before comprehensive sanctions were imposed, had a discretionary fund to disburse among organizations involved in "community outreach and leadership development." This fund is administered by the U.S. AID mission in Pretoria. AID also spends about $3 million per year on black business development, helping to train black entrepreneurs in basic skills needed to run a business; most of this money is channeled through NAFCOC (the National African Federated Chambers of Commerce), the largest black business organization in South Africa.[13]

U.S. AID is not the only government agency involved in South Africa. In 1986, the National Endowment for Democracy gave a $77,000 grant to Freedom House in New York to help black publications create a forum for discussions on democracy.[14] The Department of Commerce also has programs, one of which is sponsoring "Matchmaker Fairs," which are "designed to bring to the attention of American companies operating in South Africa the range of goods and services which they can purchase from South African non-white firms." One of the benefits of the Matchmaker Fairs is that "barriers that exist between whites and non-whites break down and [there is an] increase [of] participation of all in the mainstream of the South African economy."[15] Commerce has also aided the International Executive Service Corps in its efforts to start over thirty-five black business assistance projects.[16]

By far, however, the biggest program is the one administered by AID. From 1986 through the end of fiscal year 1988, AID "obligated $91.3 million," with a funding level for 1989 standing at $34.9 million.[17] The funds are divided among five major programs: education, human rights (including challenges to apartheid and legal defense), labor, community outreach and leadership development, and private enterprise development.

Education programs include the granting of bursaries to university students (amounting to $20 million) for study both in South Africa and in the United States and support for "a network of community based schools as models for a post-apartheid educational system, the development of a nonracial curriculum, an experimental secondary school scholarship program, training for teachers, and efforts to increase the number of blacks qualifying for university study." A total of $3.3 million is planned for these programs.[18]

Human rights expenditures are funded at $1.5 million per year and are designed to directly confront unjust apartheid laws through assistance to victims of legal action, victims of violence, and their families. It includes programs to assist those detained by the government for apartheid violations and support for challenges to the apartheid system by recourse to the judicial system.[19]

With the cooperation of the African American Labor Center, since 1983 AID has been helping black union members and leaders develop the skills necessary to operate effective labor unions. Topics of concern include organizing, collective bargaining, occupational health and safety, and grievance procedures. There is also an effort to teach union leaders to be more sensitive to the needs of a market-oriented economy. AID has also financed programs for non-union organizations in the fields of labor law, health and safety, research, and mediation and arbitration services. For 1989, AID has budgeted $1.5 million for these efforts.[20]

Since 1986, AID has been supporting community organizations so they can be more effective in their efforts to meet community needs. Projects include training for community leaders, crisis mediation, youth training and career development, and support for women. Overall expenditures on this program over a three-year period come to almost $20 million. For fiscal 1989, the amount is about $5.3 million.[21]

In the field of private enterprise development, AID has allocated a seven-year budget of $19.5 million to strengthen black business associations, provide credit to microenterprises and small businesses, and to help black businesses move into the mainstream of South Africa's industrial economy. According to AID's 1990 Congressional Presentation, "In promoting black advancement at the shop level and in the corporate boardroom, the AID program also seeks to expose blacks to the workings and values of the free market system."[22]

One of the channels for AID private enterprise assistance is the Get Ahead Foundation, which was founded in 1985 by Dr. Nthato Motlana, a Soweto physician and community leader who has been involved in anti-apartheid politics for nearly forty years. Get Ahead's budget for 1986 was $141,000 and for 1987 was $562,000. AID has given Get Ahead a grant for $1.6 million, basically doubling its program budget.[23]

Despite Dr. Motlana's background in his youth as a member of the African National Congress, which has close ties to the South African Communist Party, he has always believed in the importance of the market and the power of commercial endeavors, especially in the informal sector. According to one journalist's account, "Economic power, [Motlana] tells young political hotheads in the townships, is the flipside of political power, the one cannot do without the other. 'Go out and create wealth with your hands,' he tells young blacks."[24]

Get Ahead is consciously challenging the apartheid system. Executive director Don MacRobert said that "the Get Ahead Foundation Board believes it is wrong to deny people access to the economy on the basis of their skin color, so we get them [black businessmen] premises [in white areas]." He continued: "We believe what we do is morally and economically justifiable. We believe that the more we keep chipping away at the Group Areas Act, the more likely it is to become a dead issue."[25]

Get Ahead's board of directors is a strange mix of political activists and black entrepreneurs, including Dr. Motlana, Archbishop Desmond Tutu, Japie Moropa, and Thabo Lesolang. The Get Ahead Foundation/USA, set up to raise money for Get Ahead in the United States, has a board that includes Senator Edward Kennedy, one of the prime advocates of sanctions in the U.S. Congress, and Sal Marzullo, a Mobil Oil Company executive who has headed the Industry Support Unit, an organization that monitors the performance of U.S. companies that adhere to the Sullivan Code of equal employment principles, as well as Mpho Tutu (Archbishop Tutu's daughter) and the late Episcopal Bishop John Walker of Washington, D.C., who for a long time opposed economic sanctions but who came out in favor of them shortly before his death in 1989.

The ambiguousness of organizations such as Get Ahead, which accepts and uses AID-administered money, is but one indication of the potential controversy that comes from AID's involvement in South Africa. Armistead Lee, a former U.S.

foreign service officer with a long-standing interest in African affairs, has said that U.S. AID in South Africa has been "footdragging." They have not disbursed as much money as has been appropriated and as a result, worthy programs are going unfunded. He charged that the lack of action can be traced to staff members of the congressional committees that process legislation related to South Africa.[26] Lee suggested that these staff members thought that South African blacks should not become businessmen, because it was not befitting their status of "victims." In particular, he said, they believe that South African blacks should be "diggers of ditches and hewers of wood," not small-scale entrepreneurs.

Lee has also noted the irony of the purpose of U.S. AID policy in South Africa: AID is mandated to assist disadvantaged South Africans, who are disadvantaged precisely because U.S. imposed economic sanctions have thrown them out of work. AID is meant to ameliorate the damage caused by the U.S. Congress. Representative Dan Burton of Indiana put some figures on that perception during the markup of some proposed sanctions legislation (which was not adopted) in 1988. "Disinvestment is a discredited idea," he said. "Even radical blacks in South Africa are having second thoughts about it. American companies are widely known as the best corporate citizens in South Africa. They put over $230 million into black development; $35 million last year [1987] alone. That is more money for black development, education, housing, training, medical care, et cetera . . . than the entire U.S. AID program put into South Africa last year."[27] Even Howard Wolpe, the fervently pro-sanctions chairman of the House Subcommittee on Africa, has had to agree. During the same proceedings, he told the House Foreign Affairs Committee that "there is no question that several American firms have had exemplary records of corporate behavior in South Africa," adding that these firms "have made significant social investments in such areas as education and housing. They have, in short, improved the lives of their South African black employees."[28]

The concerns of Lee and Burton were echoed in Senate testimony presented by Jim Martin, Washington representative of the Congress of Racial Equality (CORE). He noted that AID is financing programs that were formerly funded by U.S. corporations that have since either reduced their operations in South Africa or have withdrawn completely in the face of increased economic sanctions that have raised the cost of doing business there.

Martin charged that Congress had not appropriated the full funding it had earlier authorized for AID in South Africa:

> The substitute programs to be administered by the U.S. Agency for International Development pursuant to the [Comprehensive Anti-Apartheid Act] of 1986 was funded by Congress at a level of approximately 35 percent of authorized expenditures. There was no apparent leadership by Congress to ascertain that full funding of the social responsibility programs [and] democratic catalysts occurred, it being felt that any leadership to obtain funds for the 'disadvantaged victims of apartheid' would be perceived as a desire to make apartheid 'comfortable' for those victims.[29]

He cited an additional problem: "Aid to black South Africa was compromised by the initial inter-departmental turf wars between U.S. AID and the U.S. Department of Commerce over administration of these programs."[30]

Martin's greatest concern, however, was that U.S. AID money was not going to worthwhile organizations that could do a great deal of good in terms of carrying out the original mandate of the Comprehensive Anti-Apartheid Act to assist the victims of apartheid. He noted that certain useful AID programs "seem not to be coordinated in the South African context." That is, programs that have been successful in other African countries have not been extended to South Africa to perform the same functions. Some that he mentioned included the American Schools and Hospitals Abroad Program, the Housing Guaranty Reserve Fund, the International Foundation for Electoral Assistance, the Initiative to End Hunger in Africa, the International Fund for Agricultural Development, and the Human Resources Development Assistance Project.[31] In a later conversation with the author, Martin called AID programs in South Africa "a sham and a farce."[32]

The United States is not the only country that provides assistance to South African organizations fighting apartheid through community or business development. Japan, for instance, recently raised the stakes when it announced a R1.7 million (about $850,000) grant to the Kagiso Trust, which channels funds from around the world to anti-apartheid organizations — including those linked to the African National Congress and the United Democratic Front — and to individuals, such as South African students at home and abroad.[33] The Kagiso Trust was specifically established to channel funds from abroad to non-union and non-church organizations. The European Community, too, channels its funding of community-based organizations through either the Kagiso Trust or the South African Council of Churches. EC regulations prohibit giving money directly to the organizations that will use it; hence mainstream groups such as the Urban Foundation and the Institute of Race Relations are excluded.[34]

There has been some question whether the funds received from U.S. AID and from other foreign sources are actually supporting peaceful progress in South Africa or are helping further the aims of groups that favor violent revolution. Mangosuthu Gatsha Buthelezi, chief minister of the KwaZulu homeland and leader of Inkatha, a Zulu cultural and political organization, warned in 1987:

> There was something very wrong when American dollars brought support for politics aimed at making South Africa ungovernable in tandem with the ANC's aims of developing a people's war. There is something very wrong about the formula which directs American money into South Africa to be used in this way, whereas democratic forces such as Inkatha are denied political aid.[35]

Chief Buthelezi noted that although American contributions went to the South African Council of Churches, the Congress of South African Trade Unions (COSATU), and the United Democratic Front, all these were political organizations to at least the same extent as Inkatha is. He pointed out that "American niceties about the handing over of dollars to South Africans worked only in favor of radical black organizations."[36]

Nor is Buthelezi alone in pointing up the political nature of both the donors and recipients of American (and other foreign) funds. Achmad Dangor, executive director of the Kagiso Trust, says: "There is always an agenda, whether it be the most sympathetic or the most unsympathetic foreign government. They give us the money because they want to see a certain South Africa growing out of it, one in which they will have a stake."[37]

Assessment for the Future

South Africa's apartheid problem is not going to go away. Even with the election of a new parliament on September 6, 1989, the policy of gradual reform within the context of a national state of emergency will continue. President De Klerk has, of course, indicated a greater willingness than his predecessor to negotiate with anti-apartheid organizations and to relax the emergency regulations. Despite its being outlawed for nearly thirty years, the African National Congress is operating effectively in the open in South Africa, mostly through the so-called "Mass Democratic Movement." This fluid situation may, depending upon the circumstances, either restrict U.S. AID's ability to influence events or make it a more effective player.

Because of the charged political situation inherent in South Africa, U.S. AID programs cannot avoid their political implications. AID must be on the lookout for unworthy organizations and unscrupulous persons who are seeking self-aggrandizement rather than trying to build strong communities that can resist apartheid. One unnamed anti-apartheid activist told *Tribute*, a black community magazine, complained that there is "too much" money available. "Some people," he said, "target getting their hands on this money so that they can do whatever they wish with it."[38]

U.S. AID and other donors have basically three types of organizations that can channel funds into the community. The Reverend Buti Tlhagale, director of the Educational Opportunities Council, describes them like this: The first type are "seed organizations, which are essentially non-profit-making but exist to facilitate the formation of or to support other service groups or organizations;" the second type are "enabler" organizations; the third type are political organizations and special interest groups. Examples of the first type are "Skotaville Publishers, the African Council of Hawkers and Informal Business (Achib), the recently launched Matchmaker business partnership and the National African Federated Chamber of Commerce and Industries (Nafcoc)." The second type includes the Dependents' Conference of the South African Council of Churches and the Educational Opportunities Council. The third type includes the National Educational Crisis Committee.[39]

Some South African organizations that are potential recipients of AID and other funds lack the ability to function under the same standards of accountability that most Americans would take for granted. Lebamang Sebidi of the Funda Centre in Soweto (a community education center originally built through contributions from West German corporations) admits: "Our people still do not have the cultural background for handling money; and they do not have the necessary respect for structures of accountability. . . . Our people have to be educated on how organizations and structures work. There is an appalling ignorance about how these should work. Included are things like the basics of bookkeeping as well as the necessary documents needed to run an organization."[40] A report in *Tribute* concurred with this concern: "The rush to win funding attracts petitioners whose main aim seems to be getting their hands on money. The actual projects take a back seat. Many are creating projects just because they money is there in the first place, rather than allowing existing projects to benefit."[41]

These concerns aside, it is clear that from the examples of SABTA and ACHIB, the role of the informal sector in creating the foundations for broader democracy in South Africa can be enhanced by U.S. AID assistance. Neither of these groups, however, seems to be getting any from AID, though the Center for International Private Enterprise is supporting some of their endeavor.

Even more than in Kenya, the role of the informal private sector is recognized in South Africa as having tremendous potential benefits for the society at large. Currently, however, black enterprise is confined to rather narrow sectors of the economy — transport, hawking, running "shebeens" (the nearest American equivalent is "speakeasy"). One unfortunate result is that children of successful black businessmen do not become entrepreneurs themselves but enter into prestigious professional careers. The high financial and legal costs of starting businesses prompt skilled craftsmen to take jobs with established firms — primarily white-owned — rather than starting new ones. Despite a huge increase in the building of homes for blacks who now have the right to own property, little money is going to black contractors.[42]

Still, much is being done to expand the informal sector and integrate it into the formal economy. According to Robin Friedland, "the range of activities being carried out by organizations committed to assisting black business is impressive." From the "mini-loans" disbursed by the Get Ahead Foundation to substantial loans arranged on normal commercial rates from banks or the Small Business Development Corporation, black businesses are getting helped.

Even incremental assistance from AID and other agencies can contribute significantly to small business growth. But such assistance must be provided now, before circumstances (an economic slump, a revival of Conservative Party successes and a return to old-fashioned apartheid, a rise in radical terrorist activities) prevent it. As Robin Friedland warns: "The problem of the aridity of black urban life is an enormous one: the development of black small business as a major item on the agenda for amelioration is a vast sump that will absorb the most strenuous efforts of all the field workers and more. Better that marginal effort is supplied than that too little is done where it turns out to have been needed after all."[43]

Political turmoil is a given in South Africa. Periodic riots, demonstrations, terrorist attacks, and the like continue to erode investor confidence and affect the value of the rand vis-à-vis foreign currencies. Inflation will thus remain a standard feature of the South African economy. To counter these ills, economic growth must continue at no less than 3 percent a year, although 5-6 percent will be necessary to create enough jobs to accommodate the school-leavers of the next decade. (Half of South Africa's black population is under the age of fifteen, a situation that is itself potentially explosive.)

If political reforms produce a gradual loosening of economic sanctions imposed by the West, economic growth may be expected. However, given the political complexion of the Western democracies, whose parliaments and congresses are hardly the best-informed on the facts and trends of South African politics and society and react instinctively rather than rationally when "apartheid" is mentioned, an emphasis on the carrot instead of the stick is unlikely in the future. Reforms, however significant they may be, will simply be dismissed as "cosmetic" or "too-little-too-late." In particular, economic reforms, which are probably much more important in the long run than political reforms, will be ignored because the issues are too complex to be decisive in congressional debates.

The bottom line is that South Africa has to do it itself. It has to pull itself up by its bootstraps, creating an economic climate that promotes internal prosperity (through deregulation) and invites foreign investment (despite sanctions), if not from the United States and Western Europe, then from Japan, Taiwan, South Korea, or from other countries of the Southern Hemisphere. Without economic growth, black unemployment will become unmanageable, and the dark cloud of revolutionary violence will grow ever darker. Disaffected black youth will be ripe for recruitment by the military wing of the African National Congress. However, it should be noted that the ANC has been deprived of guerrilla bases by South Africa's recent efforts at rapprochement with neighboring states, like Angola and Mozambique, that formerly were hospitable to the ANC militants. The generation now growing up surrounded by township violence will beget another generation that knows no hope. A difficult task, yes, but not impossible. As Hernando de Soto notes in his recent study of the informal economies of the Third World:

> The real remedy for violence and poverty is to recognize the property and labor of those whom formality today excludes, so that where there is rebellion there will be a sense of belonging and responsibility. When people develop a taste for independence and faith in their own efforts, they will be able to believe in themselves and in economic freedom.[44]

The economic potential of South Africa is enormous, whether we are talking about that country by itself or about South Africa as the hub of a vast economic network comprising all the countries of southern Africa, rich in human, mineral, and agricultural resources. The economic aspect of the vexing "apartheid" problem is understood far too insufficiently by American policymakers. U.S. policy toward South Africa can and should be based on facts as well as sentiment, on sound economic reasoning as well as political principles.

Notes to Chapter Eight:

[1]R. F. Botha, "The Potential and Pre-requisites for Economic Recovery in a Post-Apartheid South Africa," *Southern African Freedom Review*, Vol. 1, No. 2 (Spring 1987), p. 26.

[2]Walter H. Kansteiner, *South Africa: Revolution or Reconciliation* (Washington: Institute on Religion and Democracy, 1988), p. 4.

[3]In *The Politics of Sentiment: Churches and Foreign Investment in South Africa* (Washington: Ethics and Public Policy Center, 1984), I argue about the limits sanctions have as a tool of foreign policy. See also my "United States-South African Relations: Morality and Politics," *Vital Speeches of the Day*, October 1, 1988, pp. 761-64.

[4]Robin Friedland, "Small Business and the Informal Sector," *Optima*, Vol. 35, No. 2 (June 1987), p. 103.

[5]See Louise Tager, "Deregulation — how it only limits restrictions," *Black Enterprise* (Johannesburg), Volume 17 (1988), p. 53.

[6]See William Claiborne, "Taxis Give Blacks a Chance at the Driver's Seat," *The Washington Post*, May 18, 1988, pp. A23, A28; Knox Matjila, "The Black Transport Entrepreneur: The Next Decade," address to the National Student Federation Annual Congress, Stellenbosch, 11 July 1988; "Taximen's plans will give entrepreneurs a chance," *Black Enterprise* (Johannesburg), Volume 12 (1988), p. 33.

[7]Graciela D. Testa, "The Invisible Entrepreneurs of South Africa," *International Health and Development*, Vol 1, No. 2 (Summer 1989), p. 22.

[8]See "Hawkers' hero Lawrence has become a legend," *Black Enterprise* (Johannesburg), Volume 12 (1988), pp. 6-7.

[9]Testa, "The Invisible Entrepreneurs of South Africa," p. 23.

[10]Testimony of Ambassador Alan Keyes, *United States Policy Toward South Africa*, Hearings before the Subcomittee on African Affairs of the Committee on Foreign Relations, United States Senate, October 22, 1987, p. 44.

[11]*Proposed Economic Sanctions Against South Africa*, Hearings and Markup before the Committee on Foreign Affairs and its Subcom-

mittees on International Economic Policy and Trade, and on Africa, March 22, 23; April 20, 28; and May 3, 1988, p. 371.

[12]Ibid., p. 155.

[13]Ansophie M. Joubert, "U.S. Involvement in South Africa -- An Update," *American Review* (Institute for American Studies, Rand Afrikaans University), Vol. 8 (Second Quarter 1988), p. 3.

[14]Ibid., p. 7.

[15]Testimony of James B. Kelly, *Proposed Economic Sanctions Against South Africa,* pp. 110-11.

[16]Ibid., p. 112.

[17]U.S. Agency for International Development, *Congressional Presentation Fiscal Year 1990, Annex I, Africa,* p. 353.

[18]Ibid., p. 354.

[19]Ibid.

[20]Ibid., p. 355.

[21]Ibid.

[22]Ibid., p. 354.

[23]John D. Sullivan, unpublished memorandum, "Trip Report: Kenya, South Africa, Botswana, Nigeria, June 20 to July 2, 1988," Center for International Private Enterprise, July 30, 1988, pp. 26-28.

[24]Hellouise Truswell, "Profile: Nthato Harrison Motlana," *Optima,* Vol. 36, No. 2 (June 1988), p.89.

[25]"The aim is for blacks to Get Ahead!," *Pretoria News,* 9 April 1987.

[26]Conversation with Armistead Lee, Washington, D.C., July 31, 1989.

[27]*Proposed Economic Sanctions Against South Africa,* p. 451.

[28]Ibid., p. 509.

[29]Prepared statement of Jim Martin, *United States Policy Toward South Africa*, Hearings before the Subcomittee on African Affairs of the Committee on Foreign Relations, United States Senate, June 23, 1988, p. 553.

[30]Ibid.

[31]Ibid., pp. 554-55.

[32]Conversation with Jim Martin, Washington, D.C., July 6, 1989.

[33]"Japan opens the bidding in drive to fund anti-apartheid organisations," *SouthScan*, Vol. 4, No. 25 (June 30, 1989), p. 189.

[34]Martin Holland, *The European Community and South Africa: European Political Co-operation under Strain* (London: Pinter Publishers, 1988), pp. 118-21.

[35]Cited in Joubert, "US Involvement in South Africa," p. 12.

[36]Ibid.

[37]"Selling SA's Soul?," *Tribute* (Johannesburg), August 1989, p. 35.

[38]Ibid., p. 40.

[39]Ibid., pp. 36-37.

[40]Ibid., p. 38.

[41]Ibid., p. 40.

[42]Friedland, "Small Business and the Informal Sector", pp. 108-9.

[43]Ibid., p. 106.

[44]Hernando de Soto, *The Other Path: The Invisible Revolution in the Third World* (New York: Harper and Row, 1989), p. 258.

9

Swaziland

The last British colony in Africa to attain its independence, Swaziland is a New Jersey-size mountain kingdom of 750,000 surrounded on three sides by South Africa and on the other by Mozambique. King Sobhuza II, who took his throne at the turn of the century and died in 1982, was this century's longest-reigning monarch. His reign saw both the beginning and the end of Swaziland's status as a British protectorate, a period that began in 1903 and ended with independence in 1968.

Swaziland's main exports are sugar, wood products, fertilizer, and canned fruit. The country is rich in minerals, including iron ore, coal, and asbestos. Its rivers provide water for irrigation and hydroelectric power generation.[1] It is also heavily dependent on South Africa, where thousands of Swazis seek employment and send home more than R60 million (about $30 million) each year. South Africa receives 20 percent of Swaziland's exports and in return, 90 percent of Swaziland's imports come from South Africa, along with 50 percent of its electricity and 100 percent of its oil. Thirty-three percent of Swaziland's overseas trade is channeled through South Africa. This works both ways, however; in an effort to defeat Western consumer boycotts of South African produce, some South African exports are shipped through Swaziland and re-labelled as Swazi origin. One notable example: In a recent year, it was discovered that the volume of oranges shipped from Swaziland into the European Community equalled four times the amount of Swaziland's total orange crop.[2]

Economic Development

Swaziland has a market-oriented economy that has been characterized by stability and steady growth.[3] It is one of the handful of black African countries that is ethnically homogeneous and hence free of the inter-tribal rivalries that have bedeviled so many African states. During the 1960s, Swaziland's average annual growth rate was 8.6 percent; between 1970 and 1980 the economy grew by 4.6 percent per year.[4] It is one of only a handful of Sub-Saharan countries in which per capita food production is growing rather than declining.[5]

The Swazi government has made a genuine effort to support the private sector in both agriculture and industry, but state-run trading boards remain in place. However, independent merchandisers compete with the state marketing boards. For example, a wholesale produce market at Nokwane established in 1986 "has the novel feature that farmers can take their produce to any one of three independent agents who operate on the trading floor." Mike Dlamini, the manager of the market, which is run by the Swazi government's National Agricultural Marketing Board, insists that "having three agents creates competition and means that the farmer is more likely to get a better price."[6] Farmers seem to agree. In the first full year of operation, 1987, the market handled only 500 tons of fresh produce; in 1988, that doubled to 1,100 tons; and the estimate for 1989 is approximately 1,650 tons.[7]

At the same time, a program to assist smallholding farmers in Swaziland is encouraging the diversification of crops, many of which can command good prices across the border in South Africa. Some of those which are considered to have strong potential are broccoli, celery, garlic, ginger, leeks, parsley, and radishes. Mozambique is also becoming an export market.[8]

Development assistance from the United Nations, the European Community, and elsewhere seeks to wean Swaziland away from economic dependence on South Africa. The ties between the two countries — in terms of trade, infrastructure, and even politics — are unassailable, however. The future of Swaziland's economic development is heavily dependent on the health or weakness of South Africa.

Development consultant Robert Lincoln Hancock said in a recent interview that in Swaziland, the climate is very good for free enterprise development on a small scale. Experience shows that under some free enterprise development programs, agricultural production can double or triple within two years. Taiwan has provided significant assistance in improving agricultural productivity. And in areas of marginal agricultural production, other enterprises can be introduced (such as sewing or candlemaking); local markets for these products are identified, and these areas can then afford to buy food that they cannot grow with the income from their new enterprises.[9]

The Role of U.S. Development Aid

This is not to say that Swaziland lacks possibilities for strengthening its own economy through proper reforms and adjustments. The strategy employed by the U.S. Agency for International Development in Swaziland focuses on accelerating growth through the expansion of the private sector.[10] This support for the private sector "encompasses policy dialogue and reform, small enterprise development, and training."[11]

Private voluntary organizations (PVOs) from the United States and Swaziland are being employed by AID to provide training in small business development and to explore effective approaches for encouraging small business enterprises. AID is also providing support for the Faculty of Agriculture at the University of Swaziland so that its students will be better prepared to participate in the private agricultural sector rather than just government-supported agricultural commerce.[12]

AID is also encouraging privatization of parastatal organizations by training government employees in market-oriented techniques. AID's Manpower Project has helped establish a private enterprise monitoring unit in the Ministry of Finance to introduce market-oriented incentives.[13]

In addition, AID supports projects that are helping to expand the private agricultural sector through assistance to small-scale farmers and agribusinesses.[14]

Development consultant Robert Lincoln Hancock has criticized AID's activities in Swaziland, saying that because of budget cutbacks — about $8 million this year — AID has had to concentrate on its "pet projects" rather than grassroots, self-sustaining development programs that work.[15]

Assessment for the Future

Being a small country nearly surrounded by an economic powerhouse, Swaziland's future does not leave much room for discussion. With some 15,000 wage-earning members of its labor force more or less permanently working in South Africa, with its power-grid and transport infrastructures connected to the South African hub, and with its imports and exports not only travelling through South Africa but relying upon the Southern African Customs Union (managed by Pretoria) for the collection of tariffs and taxes, Swaziland reminds one of Pierre Trudeau's remark about Canada being like a mouse sleeping next to an elephant. When the South African elephant moves, the Swazi mouse feels more than just a rumble.

American development aid will therefore be a drop in the bucket compared to what South Africa could do, not only for Swaziland but for the southern African region as a whole, once it is freed of the apartheid incubus that has vexed southern African politics for the past forty years. Swaziland, like Botswana, Lesotho, and other neighboring states, is adversely affected by the economic sanctions imposed on South Africa by the United States and other countries. As a result of sanctions, Swazi citizens must pay higher prices for imported goods, inputs like energy are quite expensive, and the economy suffers. Since American policymakers, at least, show no inclination to lift sanctions until they are persuaded that South Africa has abandoned apartheid, the future looks bleak for Swaziland. This is despite AID's focused assistance to the member countries of the Southern Africa Development Cooperation Council (SADCC), especially in the way of finding alternative means of transportation for the member countries' mineral and other resources.[16] In the meantime, we must hope that U.S. AID will continue to encourage the development of a genuine free enterprise system in this small country shackled by adverse political circumstances beyond its control.

Notes to Chapter Nine:

[1]L. H. Gann and Peter Duignan, "Namibia, Botswana, Lesotho, and Swaziland," in Peter Duignan and Robert H. Jackson, eds., *Politics and Government in African States 1960-1985* (London: Croom Helm and Stanford, Calif.: Hoover Institution Press, 1987), p. 26.

[2]Martin Holland, *The European Community and South Africa: European Political Co-operation under Strain* (London: Pinter Publishers, 1988), p. 44.

[3]U.S. Agency for International Development, *Congressional Presentation Fiscal Year 1990, Annex I, Africa*, p. 375.

[4]Gann and Duignan, "Namibia, Botswana, Lesotho, and Swaziland," p. 373.

[5]Dunstan S. C. Spencer, "Africultural Research: Lessons of the Past, Strategies for the Future," in Robert J. Berg and Jennifer Seymour Whitaker, eds., *Strategies for African Development* (Berkeley: University of California Press, 1986), p. 215.

[6]John Madeley, "New market boosts agriculture," *African Business*, July 1989, p. 15.

[7]Ibid.

[8]Ibid., pp. 15-16.

[9]Interview with Robert Lincoln Hancock, November 29, 1989.

[10]U.S. Agency for International Development, *Congressional Presentation*, p. 375.

[11]Ibid., p. 376.

[12]Ibid., p. 377.

[13]Ibid.

[14]Ibid., pp. 376-77.

15Interview with Robert Lincoln Hancock, November 29, 1989.

16*Proposed Economic Sanctions Against South Africa*, Hearings and Markup before the Committee on Foreign Affairs and its Subcommittees on International Economic Policy and Trade, and on Africa, March 22, 23; April 20, 28; and May 3, 1988, p. 595.

10

Conclusions

The United States has had a wide variety of experiences and a wide range of successes and failures in its efforts to provide development assistance abroad. This is manifest in our examination of the seven countries in the preceding chapters: Botswana, Ivory Coast, Ghana, Kenya, Senegal, South Africa, and Swaziland. Each country has its own level of development, its own peculiar problems, its own obstacles to overcome, its own political and economic dynamics. There is no single simple solution to the development problems of sub-Saharan Africa.

To a certain extent, U.S. Agency for International Development policies proceed from this premise. Whether because of specific congressional mandates, as in the case of South Africa, or because of the influence of multilateral development banks, as seems to be the case in Ghana, U.S. AID pursues an agenda for each country as it deems appropriate. However, AID — and the World Bank and the development agencies of the European Community, Japan, and other countries — cannot give up the notion that development assistance assists development. In fact, development assistance plays a limited if not exacerbating role in the development of Third World countries — countries that were once called "backward" but are now called "developing."

The most important and perhaps only role fit for the Western development agencies is to provide the wherewithal for people in developing countries to understand their situation in a historical context and provide the bare minimum for them to take off on their own. To do more risks inducing dependency and creating the conditions not for economic progress, but for stagnation and decline.

Transactions of Decline

Most development aid programs are essentially government-to-government transfers of money. They are subsidies in much the same way, in a domestic context, Aid to Families with Dependent Children or food stamps or paying farmers not to grow certain foods are subsidies. As such, they are recipes for economic decline.

Lord Bauer, the distinguished British economist, has said quite bluntly that the receipt of foreign aid is what defines the Third World: "The Third World as an aggregate is the creation of foreign aid. Without aid, there is no such collectivity as the Third World, or South. Foreign aid is therefore the source of the North-South conflict, not its solution."[1] He derives from this thesis from this conclusion: "Aid has produced the Third World but it cannot achieve its declared purposes of development and the relief of poverty. Yet the case for foreign aid is usually taken for granted."[2]

It is taken for granted so much that the only authentically sensible course of action for Western aid agencies — to cease to exist — is politically unfeasible, almost unthinkable. People like to think they are doing good; providing development aid assists them in this. Yet they are fundamentally mistaken. Foreign private investment is much to be preferrred.

Jane Jacobs, in *Cities and the Wealth of Nations*, defines transfers of wealth from one region to another (whether internally within a country or from one foreign country to another) as "transactions of decline" that speed stagnation and decay. "Heavy and unremitting subsidies," she writes, "are transactions of decline, and once adopted the need for them grows greater with time, and the wherewithal for supplying them grows less."[3]

The growth of the development industry over the past few decades is emblematic of Jacobs' concern. Yet such growth is greeted with applause by Western policymakers, and certainly also by leaders of Third World governments who benefit personally and politically as recipients of foreign aid. As Lord Bauer put it: "Larger aid flows are described as improved aid performance. Giving more means doing better."[4] No matter how many times development officials and elected public servants repeat that assertion, it is not true. "The familiar shibboleth that aid helps people to help themselves is very nearly the complete opposite of the truth," charges Lord Bauer. "Foreign aid also tends to encourage the adoption of inappropriate external models in development and planning, often with considerable drain on the recipient country's resources."[5] This perception is shared by some Third World officials. The Swaziland minister of health has written that "donor policies today, althoug essentially and potentially beneficial, have or are contributing to: (1) failure to empower countries to set their own priorities as equal partners; (2) perpetuation of dependence as opposed to self-reliance; (3) unbalanced rather than balanced development; [and] (4) fostering the development aims of the donor rather than the country receiving assistance."[6]

It is doubtlessly compassion (among more venal political reasons) that has motivated the West to buy wholesale the view that Third World countries need subsidies to develop. "Transactions of decline have not been adopted because of a lack of concern about development," notes Jane Jacobs, "or because governments accept poverty and stagnation. On the contrary, they are meant to foster development and attack poverty." However, this has not been the case; "no matter what guise they take, [transactions of decline] are not remedies for stagnation and don't address causes of poverty."[7] In fact, these policies are based on a misunderstanding of what the causes of poverty are: Development agencies send money to poor regions because they think money fights poverty. But, as Lord Bauer insightfully points out, "Lack of money is not the *cause* of poverty: it *is* poverty. Conversely, to possess money is the *result* of economic achievement, not its *precondition*."[8]

The Road to Take

Given that development programs as commonly and currently conceived are doomed to failure and that for political reasons they are here to stay, what shape should they take? What can U.S. AID do in Africa that will not constitute a transaction of decline and will encourage genuine economic development — the achievement of prosperity?

None of the developed world — the industrialized West and Japan, to say nothing of the half-baked economies of the Communist bloc — became developed with the assistance of foreign subsidies. This evidence alone should convince any observer that development aid is not necessary for economic development. What the developed world did have was the gradual growth of conditions that make development possible, including (but this list is not exhaustive) legal regimes that respect private property, the free movement of labor, freedom to negotiate contracts, relatively low taxes and tariffs, people who were willing to work hard, and a political climate that encouraged foreign and domestic investment. Some developed countries are rich in natural resources; others are extremely poor. Some quite undeveloped countries — namely the Arab members of the Organization of Petroleum Exporting Countries — are extremely rich in resources. Saudi Arabia, in fact, is one of the largest donors of economic development aid, yet itself is an undiversified, pre-industrial, undeveloped economy (which remains an aid recipient!) in the process of trying quite hard to change. Without adoption of the legal and political circumstances that made prosperity possible in the West — and cultural strictures in this staunchly Islamic nation make such a change highly unlikely — successful economic development on the scale Saudi leaders envision is improbable.

This implies that the most useful role donor agencies can play is the transmission of the values and policy prescriptions that make democratic capitalism possible. In other words, agencies like U.S. AID should gradually be transformed from *donor* to *docent*. In the meantime, the donor agencies should play something of a watchmaker's role in the informal sectors of Third World economies.

By what do we mean a "watchmaker's role"? A watchmaker provides the gears and wheels, sets them in motion, and then leaves the watch alone. It goes by itself. So it should be with informal businesses.

In Africa, the informal economy — whether the *kalabule* of Ghana or the *jua kali* of Kenya — is booming even as formal economies stagnate. One French expert asserts that "the growth rate of the parallel economy in many African states often exceeds the expansion of the official economy, which tends to represent a decreasing share of total economic activity."[9] The informal sector has developed creative and imaginative ways to avoid the inefficiency, bottlenecks, unrealistic financial policies, foreign exchange controls, and high tariffs imposed by the official economy's bureaucratic overlords.

Peruvian novelist and politician Mario Vargas Llosa has noted this phenomenon in his own country and elsewhere in the Third World. "The informal economy," he writes, "is the people's spontaneous and creative response to the state's incapacity to satisfy the basic needs of the impoverished masses." Like the hawkers and taxi drivers of South Africa, the underground foreign exchange dealers in Ghana, and the traditional craftsmen of Senegal and Kenya, participants in the informal economy throughout Latin America and Africa are thumbing their noses at government regulations that bar them from full membership in the national economy. Vargas Llosa notes: "The informal economy — a parallel and in many ways more authentic, hardworking, and creative society than the one that hypocritically calls itself legitimate — [is] an escape hatch from underdevelopment."[10]

The informal sector can be tapped with a small expenditure of resources on the part of Western development agencies. First, through education: providing the training and skills that small-scale entrepreneurs need, with additional education provided as they move up the scale to become medium- and large-scale producers or service providers. A more important educational function, however, is persuading African elites to accept the fundamental concepts of free enterprise. Although the free market is indigenous to Africa, the idea of capitalism has been sullied by association with colonial rule. This misconception must be overcome, and education — even in the form of sophisticated "propaganda" — is the best tool for overcoming it.

Second, through one-time grants of start-up capital: In South Africa, as noted in chapter eight, a hawker needs barely $100 to get his business started. In other African countries, considerably less is necessary.

Third, assistance through private organizations to improve the associational and organizational skills of African businesses. Especially in countries other than South Africa and Zimbabwe, there is a need to help chambers of commerce and similar groups get off the ground. The exchange of information is crucial for a prosperous free-market economy; business associations facilitate the exchange of information and ideas. Such groups can also serve as a counterweight to excessive government, by providing a mediating structure that mitigates against totalitarianism.

Specific Recommendations

Some development experts argue that a radical change is necessary in U.S. development assistance. They recommend that the Agency for International Development should be abolished and a new agency should take its place. One reason is to get rid of the acronym, AID, which gives the psychological impression that "aid" — i.e., charity — is the best way to promote development. This leaves out, of course, foreign and domestic investment, "bootstraps" programs, and other non-direct-assistance methods of creating conditions for development. The Development GAP suggests that the new agency should be styled the "Administration for International Development" (no acronym change there, but the Development GAP recommends extensive restructuring of the agency).[11] Development experts Robert Berg, David Gordon, and Ralph Smuckler recommend that the restructured agency should be called "the Development Cooperation Agency," arguing that "it is timely and appropriate now to rename the agency and to redesign some aspects of its structure in order to say to all, at home and abroad, that different goals and operational style now prevail." We need to change, these analysts say, because we are moving "from an era of aid to a period stressing cooperation and mutual benefit."[12]

It may not be necessary to propose a radical restructuring — that would be far to time-consuming and could be perceived as a waste of energy that can be better invested in actual development projects — but what can U.S. AID do to help promote free enterprise and democracy in the Third World, and especially in Africa? Here are a few basic, unelaborated suggestions:

(1) In cooperation with the Congress and other executive branch agencies, AID must sort out the contradictory political agendas it either chooses or is forced to pursue. A more focused program aimed at the promotion of free enterprise with less obsequiousness towards constituencies in Congress, the media, and other development agencies can go a long way.

(2) Congress must allow AID more internal control in its hiring. Ideally, AID middle-managers and program officers who are trying to promote business growth should have some business experience. Unfortunately, current AID policy is to promote managers from within, rather than hiring people with experience from outside the agency. Because so many AID employees come to their job with a "Peace Corps" mentality — not to denigrate the Peace Corps, which as a voluntary organization does a terrific job in the trenches — and with little hands-on, practical experience in what it means to start and manage a business, they are fully unequipped to assist small businesspeople in complex and overregulated Third World settings. Personnel policies should also be more flexible, allowing AID employees to maintain their professional identities without transfiguring themselves into bureaucrats; therefore, the level of paperwork must be cut down and more emphasis placed on work in the field rather than in the headquarters in Washington.

(3) More AID money should go to "job creation" private voluntary organizations (PVOs). Private organizations, "on the ground" in their own countries, often know best how to distribute limited resources to those who have the most potential of making successes of themselves. Distant bureaucrats in capital cities — or, worse, in Washington — lack the knowledge to make decisions about proper disbursement of funds.

(4) AID should help establish more organizations around the world like the Institute for Liberty and Democracy (ILD), founded in Peru by economist-businessman Hernando de Soto. Such organizations could do the tedious legwork necessary to discover the authentic needs of the economy, particularly in the informal sector. They can seek out sources of overregulation, make recommendations for reform, and advise local businesses on means to get around red tape.

(5) Related to this, AID should arrange more conferences featuring speakers of Hernando de Soto's stature, to provide a forum at which informal sector businesspeople can communicate with each other, air grievances against their governments, discuss strategies for reform, and trade ideas for business improvement.

(6) Fundamentally, AID must work toward the indigenization of free enterprise in the Third World. Small-scale African entrepreneurs have the desire to participate in a true free market; they have the most basic skills; they understand what having free choice would mean in a liberated economy. Grassroots organizing can help overcome the cultural barriers and political ones set up by post-colonial regimes. "The key is reliable institutions at the grassroots," argues Transformation International Enterprises Robert Lincoln Hancock. Once you have an adaptable model, it can be used anywhere in the Third World. It is important to have projects that can be replicated and to meet the people where they are. This means small-scale, simple technology, none-too-complicated business concepts. It means helping the people with the basics, like simple bookkeeping, writing annual business

plans, without overshooting the genuine possibilities for success.[13]

(7) It is important to integrate efforts — among U.S. agencies, between the U.S. and international lending institutions (World Bank, IMF), and between the U.S. and other donors. As development consultant Robert Lincoln Hancock put it, "unless the agencies are dealing with an integrated approach . . . we're going to see a hodge-podge" of programs that cannot succeed. Such piecemeal humanitarian assistance — designed to make up for the shortcomings of genuine development aid — "may salve our consciences, but it doesn't solve the problem."[14]

An End to Patronizing

The attitude of Western development agencies towards the people of the Third World can best be described as patronizing. By directing development aid through governments, which for the most part have centralized economic planning and use aid money to enrich political elites rather than assist the impoverished masses, the agencies are saying the poor cannot be trusted to make decisions about their own economic well-being.

Besides being insulting, this is untrue. Even the poorest person, whether in New Delhi or New York, in Abidjan or Aberdeen, knows how to make a choice in his own best interests. As P. T. Bauer says, "Economic responsiveness does not depend on literacy or formal education. Illiterate, uneducated people can readily recognize the extension of their opportunities, they can tell whether a change makes them better or worse off, and they can certainly tell the difference between more and less."[15]

What do we seek when we seek economic growth and prosperity for the Third World? Nothing less than we seek for ourselves — security, stability, and the enabling conditions for the pursuit of happiness.[16] Or, in the words of economist Sir Arthur Lewis, himself a native of the Third World, "the advantage of economic growth is not that wealth increases happiness, but that it increases the range of human choice."[17]

Indeed, this fundamental desire for a wider range of choices is what explains the worldwide phenomenon of urbanization: people come to the cities from the countryside to seek their fortune, because they know more opportunities exist in the city than on the farm. Not only are more jobs available, but there are more goods to buy with higher wages, more people to meet, more games to play — in short, more things that add up to human happiness.

Of course, if a government chooses to circumscribe this range of choices through economic and social controls, then individuals will not be able to benefit from such a move. They do it anyway. That is why it is imperative that the free enterprise system be extended to as many countries as possible. The adoption of free markets and the values of democratic capitalism will benefit not only the poor people of the world, but also their "leaders." The poor people know this instinctively; the "leaders" have got to be taught.

Notes to Chapter Ten:

[1]Peter T. Bauer, "Creating the Third World: Foreign Aid and its Offspring," *Journal of Economic Growth,* Vol. 2, No. 4 (1987), p. 3.

[2]Ibid.

[3]Jane Jacobs, *Cities and the Wealth of Nations* (Harmondsworth, Middlesex: Penguin Books, 1986), p. 193.

[4]Bauer, "Creating the Third World," p. 3.

[5]Ibid., pp. 6-7.

[6]Fanny Friedman, M.D., "Donor Policies and Third World Health," *International Health and Development,* Vol. 1, No. 2 (Summer 1989), p. 17.

[7]Jacobs, *Cities and the Wealth of Nations,* p. 203.

[8]Bauer, "Creating the Third World," p. 6.

[9]Howard Schissel, "Second Economy Booming," *African Sunrise,* Vol. 3, No. 1 (1989), p. 6.

[10]Mario Vargas Llosa, foreword to Hernando de Soto, *The Other Path: The Invisible Revolution in the Third World* (New York: Harper and Row, 1989), pp. xiv-xv.

[11]Stephen Hellinger, Douglas Hellinger, and Fred M. O'Regan, *Aid for Just Development* (Boulder, Colo.: Lynne Rienner Publishers, 1988), pp. 75ff.

[12]"Summary of the Recommendations of the Report of the Project on Cooperation for International Development," in Robert J. Berg and David F. Gordon, *Cooperation for International Development: The United States and the Third World in the 1990s* (Boulder, Colo.: Lynne Rienner Publishers, 1989), p. 336.

[13]Interview with Robert Lincoln Hancock, Transformation International Enterprises, November 29, 1989.

[14]Ibid.

[15]P. T. Bauer, "Market Order and State Planning in Economic Development," *Journal of Economic Growth*, Vol. 1, No. 1 (1986), p. 8.

[16]*See* Charles Murray, *In Pursuit: Of Happiness and Good Government* (New York: Simon and Schuster, 1988).

[17]W. Arthur Lewis, *The Theory of Economic Growth* (1955), cited by Bauer, "Market Order and State Planning," p. 5.

Bibliography

Books:

Bauer, P. T. *Equality, the Third World, and Economic Delusion.* Cambridge, Mass.: Harvard University Press, 1981.

Berg, Robert J., and Gordon, David F., eds. *Cooperation for International Development: The United States and the Third World in the 1990s.* Boulder, Colo.: Lynne Rienner Publishers, 1989.

Berg, Robert J., and Whitaker, Jennifer Seymour, eds. *Strategies for African Development.* Berkeley, Calif.: University of California Press, 1986.

Berger, Peter L., and Godsell, Bobby, eds. *A Future South Africa: Visions, Strategies, and Realities.* Cape Town: Human & Rousseau Tafelberg, 1988.

Berger, Peter L., and Neuhaus, Richard John. *To Empower People: The Role of Mediating Structures in Public Policy.* Washington: American Enterprise Institute, 1977.

Briand, Michael, ed. *Dialogue in Williamsburg: The Turning Point for South Africa?.* San Francisco: Institute for Contemporary Studies, 1989.

Butler, Jeffrey; Elphick, Richard; and Welsh, David, eds. *Democratic Liberalism in South Africa: Its History and Prospect.* Middletown, Conn.: Wesleyan University Press, 1987.

Carter, Gwendolen M., and O'Meara, Patrick, eds. *International Politics in Southern Africa.* Bloomington, Ind.: Indiana University Press, 1982.

Coffin, Frank M. *Witness for AID.* Boston: Houghton Mifflin Company, 1964.

De Silva, Donatus, et al. *Against All Odds: Breaking the Poverty Trap.* Cabin John, Md.: Seven Locks Press and Alexandria, Va.: The Panos Institute, 1989.

De Soto, Hernando. *The Other Path: The Invisible Revolution in the Third World.* New York: Harper and Row, 1989.

Douglas, William A. Developing Democracy. Washington: Heldref Publications, 1972.

Downs, R. E., and Reyna, S. P., eds. *Land and Society in Contemporary Africa.* Hanover, N.H.: University Press of New England, 1989.

Duignan, Peter, and Jackson, Robert H., eds. *Politics and Government in African States, 1960-1985.* Stanford, Calif.: Hoover Institution Press and London: Croom Helm, 1986.

Friedman, Milton. *Capitalism and Freedom.* Chicago: University of Chicago Press, 1962.

Goldman, Ralph M., and Douglas, William A., eds. *Promoting Democracy.* New York: Praeger Publishers, 1988.

Harris,. Myles. *Breakfast in Hell: A Doctor's Experiences of the Ethiopian Famine.* London: Picador, 1986.

Hayes, J. P. *Economic Effects of Sanctions on Southern Africa.* London: Trade Policy Research Centre and Gower Publishing Company, 1987.

Hellinger, Stephen; Hellinger, Douglas; and O'Regan, Fred M. *Aid for Just Development.* Boulder, Colo.: Lynne Rienner Publishers, 1988.

Hemming, Richard, and Mansoor, Ali M. *Privatization and Public Enterprises.* Occasional Paper 56. Washington: International Monetary Fund, 1988.

Holland, Heidi. *The Struggle: A History of the African National Congress.* New York: George Braziller, Inc., 1990.

Holland, Martin. *The European Community and South Africa: European Political Co-operation under Strain.* London and New York: Pinter Publishers, 1988.

Jacobs, Jane. *Cities and the Wealth of Nations: Principles of Economic Life.* Harmondsworth, Middlesex, England: Penguin Books, 1986.

Johnson, Paul.. *Modern Times: The World fom the Twenties to the Eighties.* New York: Harper and Row, 1983.

Kalyalya, Denny; Mhlanga, Khethiwe; Seidman, Ann; and Semboya, Joseph, eds. *Aid and Development in Southern Africa: Evaluating a Participatory Learning Process.* Trenton, N.J.: Africa World Press, 1988.

Kennedy, Paul. *African Capitalism: The Struggle for Ascendency.* Cambridge: Cambridge University Press, 1988.

Lal, Deepak. *The Poverty of 'Development Economics.'* Cambridge, Mass.: Harvard University Press, 1985.

Linowes, David F. *Privatization: Toward More Effective Government.* Champaign, Ill.: University of Illinois Press, 1988.

Lipton, Merle. *Capitalism and Apartheid.* Totowa, N.J.: Rowman & Allanheld, 1985.

Market-Oriented Paths To Economic Growth: Lessons of the 1980s. Washington: Center for International Private Enterprise, 1989.

Montgomery, John D. *The Politics of Foreign Aid.* New York: Frederick A. Praeger, 1962.

Murray, Hugh, ed. *The High Road.* Cape Town: Argus Leadership Publications, 1987.

Nasser, Martin E., et al. *Wealth Creation in South Africa: Strategies for Economic Freedom and Growth in the 90s.* Pretoria: Project Free Enterprise/University of South Africa, 1989.

Novak, Michael. *The Spirit of Democratic Capitalism.* New York: Simon and Schuster, 1982.

Obasanjo, Olusegun. *Africa in Perspective: Myths and Realities.* New York: Council on Foreign Relations, 1987.

Pfeffermann, Guy P. *Private Business in Developing Countries: Improved Prospects.* International Finance Corporation, Discussion Paper Number 1. Washington: The World Bank, 1988.

Serageldin, Ismail. *Poverty, Adjustment, and Growth in Africa.* Washington: The World Bank, 1989.

Sincere, Richard E., Jr. *The Politics of Sentiment: Churches and Foreign Investment in South Africa.* Washington: Ethics and Public Policy Center, 1987.

Sinclair, Michael. *Community Development in South Africa: A Guide for American Donors.* Washington: Investor Responsibility Research Center, 1986.

Sithole, Ndabaningi. *The Secret of American Success, Africa's Great Hope.* Washington: Gazaland Publishers, 1988.

Sullivan, John D., ed. *Building Constituencies for Economic Change: Report on the International Conference on the Informal Sector.* Washington: Center for International Private Enterprise, 1987.

Vugar, Sanford J. *Africa: The People and the Politics of an Emerging Continent.* New York: Simon and Shuster, 1985.

Williams, Walter E. *South Africa's War Against Capitalism.* New York: Praeger Publishers, 1989.

Zulu, Justin B., and Nsouli, Saleh M. *Adjustment Programs in Africa: The Recent Experience.* Occasional Paper 34. Washington: International Monetary Fund, 1988.

Government Documents:

Agency for International Development, U.S. *Congressional Presentation, Fiscal Year 1990, Annex I, Africa,* n.d. (1989).

Agency for International Development, U.S. *Development and the National Interest: U.S. Economic Assistance into the 21st Century,* February 1989.

Agency for International Development, *U.S. Economic Growth and the Third World: A Report on the AID Private Enterprise Initiative.* Washington: USAID, April 1987.

General Accounting Office, U.S. *Economic Assistance: Ways to Reduce the Reprogramming Notification Burden and Improve Congressional Oversight*, September 1989.

General Accounting Office, U.S. *Foreign Aid: Problems and Issues Affecting Economic Assistance*, December 1988.

General Accounting Office, U.S. *South Africa: Enhancing Enforcement of the Comprehensive Anti-Apartheid Act*, July 1989.

Government Accounting Office, U.S. South Africa: *Status Report on Implementation of the Comprehensive Anti-Apartheid Act*, October 1987.

House of Representatives, U.S. *Background Materials on Foreign Assistance*. Report of the Task Force on Foreign Assistance to the Committee on Foreign Affairs, February 1989.

House of Representatives, U.S. *Proposed Economic Sanctions Against South Africa*. Hearings and Markup before the Committee on Foreign Affairs and its Subcommittees on International Economic Policy and Trade, and on Africa, March 22, 23; April 20, 28; and May 3, 1988.

House of Representatives, U.S. *Report of the Task Force on Foreign Assistance to the Committee on Foreign Affairs*, February 1989.

House of Representatives, U.S. *Structural Adjustment in Africa: Insights from the Experiences of Ghana and Senegal*. Report of a Staff Study Mission to Great Britain, Ghana, Senegal, Cote d'Ivoire, and France, Nov. 29-Dec. 20, 1988, to the Committee on Foreign Affairs, March 1989.

House of Representatives, U.S. *The President's Report on Progress Toward Ending Apartheid in South Africa and the Question of Future Sanctions*. Hearing before the Subcommittees on International Economic Policy and Trade, and on Africa of the Committee on Foreign Affairs, November 5, 1987.

Senate, U.S. *Security and Development Assistance*. Hearings before the Committee on Foreign Relations, Parts 1 and 2, February 24, 25, and 26 and March 10, 12, 16, 23, 25, and 26, 1987.

Senate, U.S. *The United States in a Global Economy.* Hearings before the Committee on Foreign Relations, February 27, 28, and March 6, 1985.

Senate, U.S. *United States Policy Toward South Africa.* Hearings before the Subcommittee on African Affairs of the Committee on Foreign Relations, October 22, 1987, and June 22, 23, and 24, 1988.

Articles:

Alexander, Gerard. "African Success Stories: Democracy and Free Enterprise in Five African Nations," *Policy Review,* Spring 1986.

Ayittey, George B. N. "A Blueprint for African Economic Reform," *Journal of Economic Growth,* Vol. 2, No. 3 (1987).

Ayittey, George B. N. "Africa's Agricultural Disaster: Governments and Elites Are to Blame," *Journal of Economic Growth,* Vol. 1, No. 3 (1986).

Ayittey, George B. N. "Restoring Africa's Free Market Tradition," *Backgrounder* (The Heritage Foundation), No. 661 (July 6, 1988).

Ayittey, George B. N. "The Political Economy of Reform in Africa," *Journal of Economic Growth,* Vol. 3, No. 3 (Spring 1989).

Ayittey, George B. N. "Why Can't Africa Feed Itself?," *International Health and Development,* Vol. 1, No. 2 (Summer 1989).

Bauer, Peter T. "Creating the Third World: Foreign Aid and Its Offspring," Journal of Economic Growth, Vol. 2, No. 4 (1987).

Berg, Elliot. "Private Sector Potential in Africa," *Journal of Economic Growth,* Vol. 1, No. 3 (1986).

Bethlehem, Ronald. "Social Accord," *Leadership South Africa,* Vol. 8, No. 3 (1989).

Bissell, Richard E. "The Pursuit of Coherence," *Orbis,* Vol. 25, No. 4 (Winter 1982).

Bovard, James. "The World Bank's Structural Adjustment Loans," *Journal of Economic Growth*, Vol. 2, No. 3 (1987).

Cadorette, Curt. "Enterprising Spirit as Saving Grace," *The World & I*, Vol. 4, No. 6 (June 1989).

Cardoso, Eliana A. "Wrong Way," *The World & I*, Vol. 4, No. 6 (June 1989).

Catley-Carlson, Margaret. "Aid: A Canadian Vocation," in Stephen R. Graubard, ed., *In Search of Canada*. New Brunswick, N.J.: Transaction Publishers, 1989.

Clark, Andrew. "Quiet Revolution: South Africa's Blacks Are Realizing Their Economic Power," *Reason*, July 1989.

"Development and Peace: An Illusory Link?" *In Brief . . .* (United States Institute of Peace), Number 7, July 1989.

Eberstadt, Nicholas. "Poverty in South Africa," *Optima*, Vol. 36, No. 1 (March 1988)

Eberstadt, Nick. "Four Myths about Africa," *The National Interest*, Winter 1987/88.

Feige, Edgar L. "The (Underground) Wealth of Nations," *The World & I*, Vol. 4, No. 6 (June 1989).

Friedland, Robin. "Small Business and the Informal Sector," *Optima*, Vol. 35, No. 2 (June 1987).

Friedman, Fanny. "Donor Policies and Third World Health," *International Health and Development*, Vol. 1, No. 2 (Summer 1989).

Fukuyama, Francis. "The End of History?," *The National Interest* 16, Summer 1989.

Harsch, Ernest. "After Adjustment," *Africa Report*, May-June 1989.

Holmes, Michael. "Diamonds and Dust," *Leadership South Africa*, Vol 6, No. 4 (1987).

Kantor, Brian. "Economic and Political Freedom in South Africa: The Role of the Informal Sector," *Southern African Freedom Review*, Vol. 1, No. 4 (Fall 1988).

Kedourie, Elie. "The State as Smothering Mama," *The World & I*, Vol. 4, No. 6 (June 1989).

Kenney, Henry. "South Africa and the Stages of Growth," *Optima*, Vol. 35, No. 2 (June 1987).

Kraus, Jon. "Revolution and the Military in Ghana," *Current History*, March 1983.

Landes, David. "Rich Country, Poor Country," *The New Republic*, November 20, 1989.

Ndegwa, Philip. "National Policies for Balanced and Sustainable Development in the Poor Countries," *Development: Journal of the Society for International Development*, No. 1 (1989).

Nickel, Herman. "Promoting Change in South Africa," *SAIS Review*, Vol. 8, No. 1 (Winter-Spring 1988).

Nicolaides, Philip. "Black Marketeers Unite!," *The World & I*, Vol. 4, No. 6 (June 1989).

Sincere, Richard E. "Black Market Forcing African States To Curtain Economic Restrictions," *New York City Tribune*, July 17, 1989.

Sincere, Richard E. "Helping Build a Postapartheid South Africa," *The World & I*, Vol 4, No. 12 (December 1989).

Sincere, Richard E. "United States-South African Relations: Morality and Politics," *Vital Speeches of the Day*, October 1, 1988.

Sorzano, José S. "The Revenge of the Invisible Hand," *The World & I*, Vol. 4, No. 6 (June 1989).

Stamp, Patricia. "Kenya's Year of Discontent," *Current History*, March 1983.

Stokeld, Frederick W. "Africa and Foreign Aid: Using Scarce Resources Wisely," *Orbis*, Vol. 25, No. 4 (Winter 1982).

Tammen, Melanie S. "The Failure of State Agriculture in Sub-Saharan Africa," *Journal of Economic Growth,* Vol. 3, No. 2 (November 1988).

Tammen, Melanie S. "World Bank Sows Bad Advice in Africa," *The Wall Street Journal,* April 13, 1988.

Testa, Graciela D. "The Invisible Entrepreneurs of South Africa," *International Health and Development,* Vol. 1, No. 2 (Summer 1989).

Wick, Pascal. "The Role of Government in the Economic Recession of Cote d'Ivoire," *Journal of Economic Growth,* Vol. 3, No. 3 (Spring 1989).

Zinsmeister, Karl. "East African Experiment: Kenyan Prosperity and Tanzanian Decline," *Journal of Economic Growth,* Vol 2, No. 2 (1987).

Publisher's Note

The International Freedom Foundation is a Washington-headquartered non-profit educational foundation which has been recognized by the Internal Revenue Service as a tax-exempt organization. IFF has branch offices in London, Hamburg, Paris, Brussels, and Johannesburg. Through a variety of activities (see partial listing below) IFF promotes individual liberty, free market principles, and the building of truly democratic institutions.

Endeavoring to promote thorough and balanced public debate on foreign policy issues IFF has successfully completed the following projects:

SOUTHERN AFRICA:

South Africa: IFF has conducted an extensive campaign, through our office in Johannesburg, to encourage an end to apartheid and the establishment of a constitutional order in South Africa in which individual rights and economic freedom will be protected. The Foundation has effectively promoted the concept of black economic empowerment as a means of breaking down the apartheid system.

Angola: The International Freedom Foundation vigorously demonstrated the need for national reconciliation to end the civil war in Angola. In December of 1988, in conjunction with the Graduate School of International Studies at the University of Miami, the Foundation sponsored a two-day conference on the Angola-Namibia negotiations, which was addressed by leading African, Soviet, Cuban, and American experts on the region, including Dr. Henry Kissinger. IFF publishes *Angola Peace Monitor*, a newsletter which analyses developments in the Angolan peace process.

Namibia: IFF sponsored an international observer mission to the Namibian elections, which included parliamentarians from Britain, Germany, Belgium, and the United States.

WESTERN HEMISPHERE:

Nicaragua: The International Freedom Foundation organized and mobilized some 35,000 Nicaraguan exiles and refugees living outside of Nicaragua in a petition drive designed to secure their right to vote in the February 25 Nicaraguan elections. IFF sponsored a trip to Britain and Germany by Armando Zambrana, a United Nicaraguan Opposition candidate for the National Assembly, to inform the people of Europe about issues in the Nicaraguan election.

Cuba: IFF sponsored a U.S.-Cuba Roundtable in September 1987 which was addressed by leading Cuban defectors, academics and policy professionals who examined Cuba's domestic and foreign policies as well as the question of normalization of U.S.-Cuban relations.

Panama: Beginning in February 1988, IFF has been a leader in demonstrating the need for a re-evaluation of U.S. policy toward Panama. The Foundation sponsored an extensive study of the constitutionality of the Panama Canal Treaties, and collected over 100,000 petitions to the President urging reconsideration of the treaties. IFF sent a mission to observe the elections of May 1989; and sponsored a Roundtable discussion with congressman from both parties, former diplomats, and military and public policy experts to suggest a U.S. response to the voiding of those elections. IFF is currently studying ways that the United States can prevent the rise of another Noriega in Panama.

Chile: The International Freedom Foundation sent a mission to observe the conduct of the November 1988 plebiscite and continues to monitor the country's return to democratic rule.

EUROPE:

EEC: IFF is currently engaged in a major European development initiative, designed to develop contacts with the leaders of major western European governments, as well as the emerging European bureaucracy.

Eastern Europe: Through the Foundation's office in Hamburg, IFF is closely studying the rapidly changing face of eastern Europe. IFF is conducting an extensive program of education to encourage the development of free market political parties in East Germany and other emerging democracies.

ORIGINAL RESEARCH:

Soviet Studies: The International Freedom Foundation is co-sponsoring, with the Council for Inter-American Security, a project by Dr. John Lenczowski, Soviet Affairs analyst in President Reagan's National Security Council, to study political influence operations by the Soviet Union in the West. IFF expects to publish the results of the research in early 1991.

PUBLICATIONS:

Freedom Bulletin: a monthly newsletter which focuses on the work of the Foundation and developments in the advancement of freedom worldwide. Additional editions are produced by the Foundation's branch offices which focus on issues of regional interest.

International Freedom Review: our quarterly policy journal, which features articles by leading academics and government leaders on issues of global significance.

European Freedom Review: a quarterly journal, produced in London, which looks at foreign policy issues from a British perspective.

Southern African Freedom Review: A quarterly journal of political and economic theory and analysis on issues facing southern Africa.

Publications are available from:

International Head Office
IFF (USA)
200 G Street, N.E. , Suite 300
Washington, D.C. 20002
United States of America

IFF (UK)
10 Storey's Gate, Westminster
London, SW1P 3AY
United Kingdom

IFF (Benelux)
Post Box 2, 22
Brussels 1000
Belgium

IFF (Germany)
Ritterstrasse 16
Buxtehude 2150
Federal Republic of Germany

IFF(France)
38, rue de Berri
Paris 75007
France

IFF (RSA)
Post Box 67926
Bryanston 2021
Republic of South Africa